INTERMEDIATE

ROCK GUITAR

The Complete Rock Guitar Method

Beginning · Intermediate · Mastering

PAUL HOWARD

Alfred, the leader in educational publishing, and the National Guitar Workshop, one of America's finest guitar schools, have joined forces to bring you the best, most progressive educational tools possible. We hope you will enjoy this book and encourage you to look for other fine products from Alfred and the National Guitar Workshop.

Acquisition, editorial, music typesetting and internal design: Nathaniel Gunod, Workshop Arts
Photo acquisition: Mike Allain, Workshop Arts
CD recorded and engineered by Mark Dziuba, Workshop Sounds, New Paltz, NY
Consulting editors: Link Harnsberger and Ron Manus, Alfred Publishing
Cover photo: Jeff Oshiro • Cover design: Ted Engelbart/Martha Widmann

TABLE OF CONTENTS

ABOUT THE AUTHOR

Paul Howard has been a guitar instructor and performer for over twenty years. His experience includes rock, country, folk and jazz on both acoustic and electric guitar. He began private teaching in 1970 and graduated with honors from Central Connecticut State University in 1972. Paul has been a faculty member at the National Guitar Summer Workshop since its inception in 1984. He also operates his own music school in Avon, Connecticut. Paul released two albums with his band, Last Fair Deal, and can be seen playing around New England with the Paul Howard Group. He also tours nationally with the Stacy Phillips/Paul Howard Duo.

DEDICATION
This book is dedicated to all of my students, who, over the years, have taught me much about music and about life. And to my parents, Dorothy and Irving Howard, who encouraged my musical endeavors every step of the way.

ACKNOWLEDGMENTS
Special thanks to: David Smolover, Lou Manzi, Nat Gunod, Miriam Davidson, Ken Parille, Karen Howard and all of my colleagues at the National Guitar Summer Workshop.

INTRODUCTION

This book is the culmination of a lifetime of teaching, observing, studying, listening and playing the guitar. In the following pages you will find the essential information that you need as a rock guitarist.

My experiences working with hundreds of students over the years have influenced the order and content of *Intermediate Rock Guitar*. Use this book in a progressive manner—from chapter to chapter. Occasionally, go back to review old material. Everything you have learned since studying it the first time will give you a new perspective. The book can be used with or without an instructor, but the advice and encouragement of a good teacher should not be underestimated.

Good practice is important. Learn all the exercises slowly and carefully, working up speed gradually. Slow and correct is better than fast and sloppy. Assess your progress by choosing a note, and from that note, play every scale, chord, arpeggio, lick and noise that you know. If you have a problem, try to categorize it as either technique, rhythm or understanding. Technical problems should be worked out very slowly. Difficult rhythms should be clapped while tapping your foot. Problems of understanding can be solved with your teacher or by carefully studying this book.

Expand on the sample licks provided in this book with your own variations. Remember that things can be done many ways on the guitar. When you are ready, spend time learning to solo over the example progressions. Use the CD that is available for this book, or tape yourself playing rhythm, maybe with a drum machine, and solo over the playback. Also, checkout some of the play-along practice tapes on the market, such as the *Stand Alone Tracks* series published by The National Guitar Workshop and Alfred.

Rhythm is the single most important element of music. Always work on your "feel" and timing. Try playing drums to work on the rhythmic independence of the different parts of your body. Slapping your knee and tapping your foot works great, too! It is important to work with a metronome or drum machine to improve your sense of rhythm.

Jam with as many people as you can: people who can blow you away, people who can't keep up with you and especially people from whom you can learn.

There is no substitute for training your ear. It is your ear that will tell you what is—and isn't—working in your playing. Sing. Singing connects your ear to your brain and, in turn, your brain to your fingers. Never forget that.

Learn to read music. It is a language understood by musicians all over the world, regardless of the instrument they play. Tablature is great too, and, combined with standard notation, provides the most complete guitar information.

There is no place for narrow-minded people in the world of music. Seek out advice from other players, friends and idols. Find a good private instructor to unlock new doors for you. There is great music in every style. Listen to it all: rock, jazz, folk, country, classical and all the different categories of each. The legacy of wonderful music left by the musicians of the past is your foundation. Be a team player in a band and bare your soul as a soloist. Above all have fun, develop a positive attitude and let playing music take its rightful place as one of the most rewarding experiences of your life.

CHAPTER 1

Getting Started

This chapter introduces the basic information that is essential for both understanding the guitar and communicating with other musicians. Like any field of endeavor, music has a vocabulary and a system that makes this understanding and communication easier. If you mastered this material in *Beginning Rock Guitar*, you can skip this chapter and go on to Chapter 2.

Music is a language. Its alphabet is simple. It has only seven letters that are repeated again and again: A - B - C - D - E - F - G - A - B - C, etc. Each letter represents a musical sound of a specific *pitch* (highness or lowness). We call these sounds *notes*. Note names repeat every eight steps through the alphabet. The distance from a note to the next note with the same name is called an *octave*.

THE GUITAR FINGERBOARD

HALF STEPS AND WHOLE STEPS
Our first order of business is to understand how the guitar fingerboard works and to learn how to find or name all of these notes on the neck. This is easy if we know about *half steps* and *whole steps*.

A half step is the distance from one fret to the next on the guitar. For instance, the distance from the 1st fret to the 2nd is one half step. This is the smallest *interval* (distance between two notes). Two half steps equal one whole step, which is a distance of two frets on the guitar. For instance, the distance from the 1st fret to the 3rd fret is a whole step.

The arrangement of whole steps and half steps in the musical alphabet is as follows:

∨ and W = Whole step
‿ and H = Half step

Here is where all of the notes in the musical alphabet —the *natural notes*—are found on the guitar.

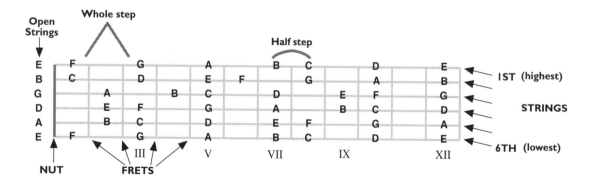

You have probably noticed the blank, unnamed frets on the fingerboard in the diagram on page 6. These are filled with *sharp* and *flat* notes, also called *accidentals* or *chromatic tones*. When a sharp ♯ is placed in front of a note, the note is raised one half step (one fret). For example, F♯ is one fret higher than F. When a flat ♭ is placed in front of a note, the note is lowered one half step (one fret). For example, G♭ is one fret lower than G. You will notice that F♯ and G♭ fall on the same fret. Two notes which sound the same (played on the same fret), but are given different letter names, are called *enharmonic equivalents*. Every sharped or flatted note has an enharmonic equivalent.

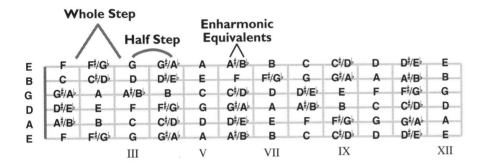

THE CHROMATIC SCALE

The chromatic scale contains all of the natural and chromatic tones. It is composed of half steps. Familiarity with this scale will help you learn the notes on the neck.

A	A♯ or B♭	B	C	C♯ or D♭	D	D♯ or E♭	E	F	F♯ or G♭	G	G♯ or A♭

As you can see, the distance from one note to the next in this scale is always one half step. Also, if you start at any point and count up twelve half steps, you will arrive on the same note name you started with. There are twelve half steps in an octave.

Here is an example of how you can use this information to learn the notes on the guitar:

What note is on the 6th fret of the 6th string?
Refer to the fingerboard chart above. The open 6th string is an E. Find E in the chromatic scale and count up six half steps (six frets) starting with F (the note after E). You will arrive at the 6th fret and A♯/B♭. Remember, every chromatic note has two names.

TUNING

Track 1

There are many ways to get the guitar into standard tuning. Most beginning players tune by comparing the open string to the 5th fret of the next lower string. This works for every string except the 2nd string. To tune the 2nd string, compare it to the 4th fret of the 3rd string.

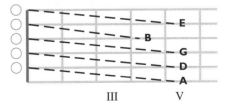

Use a tuning fork or piano to make sure you are tuning to standard concert pitch (A440)*. Tuning can be greatly simplified by using an electronic tuner, but it is important to train your ear. Every musician must be able to hear when their instrument is out of tune.

*Some musicians and bands prefer to tune one half step lower, or even a whole step lowe,r than concert pitch.

MUSIC NOTATION

For purposes of communication, some knowledge of standard musical notation and the most common terminolgy is needed. Nowadays, there are many books and magazines containing educational material and popular rock songs for guitarists. (I wish all of that was available when I was starting out!) If you want to be able to read the arrangements and examples in the books, then this information is for you.

PITCH

Notes
Music is written by placing notes on a *staff*. Notes appear various ways.

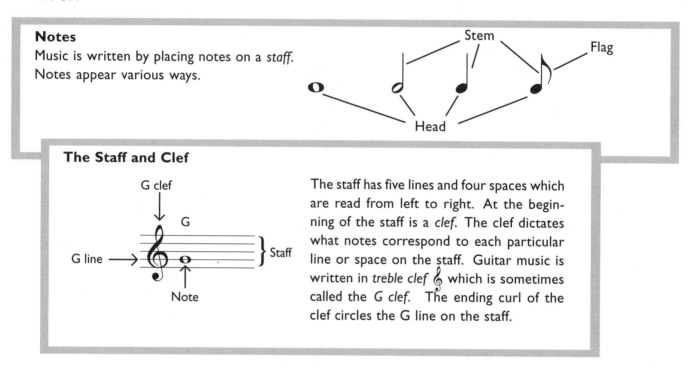

The Staff and Clef

The staff has five lines and four spaces which are read from left to right. At the beginning of the staff is a *clef*. The clef dictates what notes correspond to each particular line or space on the staff. Guitar music is written in *treble clef* which is sometimes called the *G clef*. The ending curl of the clef circles the G line on the staff.

Here are the notes on the staff using the G clef:

Ledger Lines
The higher a note appears on the staff, the higher it sounds. When a note is too high or too low to be written on the staff, *ledger lines* are used.

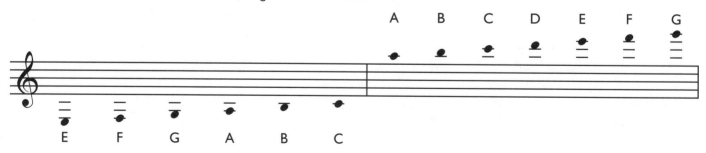

Guitar music actually sounds one octave lower than it is written. We write the music an octave higher than it sounds strictly for reasons of convenience and easy reading.

TIME

Measures and Bar Lines

The staff is divided by vertical lines called *bar lines.* The space between two bar lines is called a *measure.* Measures divide music into groups of *beats.* A beat is an equal division of time. Beats are the basic pulse behind music. A *double bar* marks the end of a section or example.

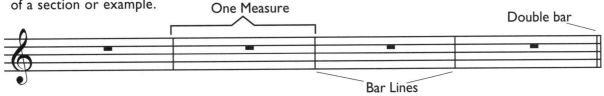

One Measure

Double bar

Bar Lines

Note Values

As you know, the location of a note relative to the staff tells us its pitch (how high or how low it is). The duration, or value, is indicated by its shape.

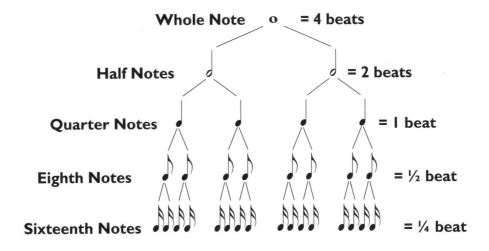

Whole Note ○ = 4 beats

Half Notes = 2 beats

Quarter Notes = 1 beat

Eighth Notes = ½ beat

Sixteenth Notes = ¼ beat

Time Signatures

Every piece of music has numbers at the beginning that tell us how to count time. The top number represents the number of beats per measure. The bottom number represents the type of note receiving one count.

4 ◄ 4 beats per measure
4 ◄ Quarter note ♩ = one beat

3 ◄ 3 beats per measure
4 ◄ Quarter note ♩ = one beat

6 ◄ 6 beats per measure
8 ◄ Eighth note ♪ = one beat

Sometimes a 𝄴 is written in place of 4/4. This is called *common time.*

Rest Values

Every note value has a corresponding rest. A rest indicates silence. A whole rest indicates four beats of silence, a half rest is two beats of silence, etc.

▬ = Whole rest, 4 beats

▬ = Half rest, 2 beats

𝄽 = Quarter rest, one beat

𝄾 = Eighth rest, ½ beat

𝄿 = Sixteenth rest, ¼ beat

Ties

When notes are tied, the second note is not struck. Rather, its value is added to that of the first note. So, a half note tied to a quarter note would equal three beats.

Notice the numbers under the staff in these examples. They indicate how to count. Both of these examples are in $\frac{4}{4}$ time, so we count four beats in each measure. When there are eighth notes, which are only ½ beat, we count "&" ("and") to show the division of the beats into two parts. When a counting number is in parenthases, a note is being held rather than struck.

Ties are a convenient way to notate notes that begin off the beat (on an "&").

Consecutive eighth notes are *beamed* together. See page 11.

Dots

A dot increases the length of a note by one half of its original value. For instance, a half note equals two beats. Half of its value is one beat (a quarter note). So a dotted half note equals three beats (2 + 1 = 3). A dotted half note is equal to a half note tied to a quarter note.

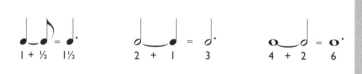

Dotted notes are especially important when the time signature is $\frac{3}{4}$ time, because the longest note value that will fit in a measure is a dotted half note. Also, dotted notes are very important in $\frac{6}{8}$ time, because not only is a dotted half note the longest possible note value, but a dotted quarter note is exactly half of a measure (counted 1 & ah 2 & ah).

Triplets

A triplet is a group of three notes that divides a beat (or beats) into three equal parts.

Eighth-Note Triplet
(evenly divides one beat)

Quarter-Note Triplet
(evenly divides two beats)

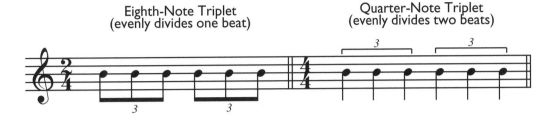

Beaming

Notes that are less than one beat in duration are often beamed together. Notice the counting numbers: since there are four sixteenth notes in a beat, they are counted "1 e & ah 2 e & ah," etc.

Beamed eighth notes

1 & 2 & 3 & 4 &

Beamed sixteenth notes

1 e & ah 2 e & ah

Rhythmic Notation

Rhythmic notation is common in guitar music. It is a system of slash marks with stems and beams that notate specific rhythms without specific pitches. Rhythmic notation is usually used to show a rhythm guitar part.

Whole Notes (4 beats)   Half notes (2 beats)

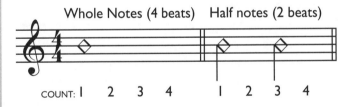

COUNT: 1   2   3   4   1   2   3   4

Quarter notes (1 beat)   Eighth notes (½ beat)

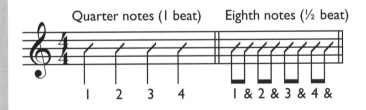

1   2   3   4   1 & 2 & 3 & 4 &

Swing Eighths

Rock music, especially blues oriented rock music, frequently sounds a bit different than notated. The *swing* or *shuffle* rhythm is very commonly played even when regular *straight eighths* are written. *Swing eighths* sound very much like eighth note triplets with a tie between the first two notes in the triplet.

Swing Eighths

Sound like this...   ...but look like this.

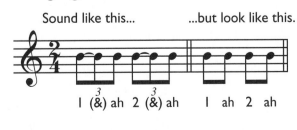

1 (&) ah 2 (&) ah   1 ah 2 ah

TAB

Tablature is a system of notation that graphically represents the strings and frets of the guitar fingerboard. Each note is indicated by placing a number, which indicates the fret to play, on the appropriate string.

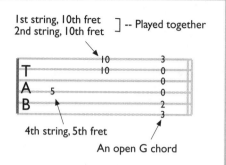

1st string, 10th fret
2nd string, 10th fret] -- Played together

4th string, 5th fret

An open G chord

Scale Diagrams

The top line of a scale diagram represents the 1st (highest) string of the guitar, and the bottom line the 6th string. The vertical lines represent frets, which are numbered with Roman numerals.

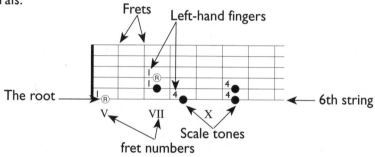

Frets   Left-hand fingers

The root

V   VII   X   6th string

Scale tones

fret numbers

Chord Diagrams

Chord diagrams are similar to scale diagrams, except they are oriented vertically instead of horizontally. Vertical lines represent strings, and horizontal lines represent frets. Roman numerals are used to number the frets.

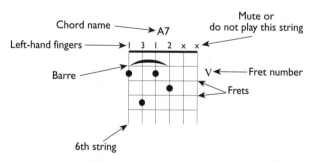

Chord name   →   A7   Mute or do not play this string

Left-hand fingers   →   1 3 1 2 x x

Barre   V ← Fret number

Frets

6th string

Here is a review of Roman numerals and their Arabic equivalents.

I .....i 1	IV ..iv .. 4	VII .....vii . 7	X ....x 10	XIII ... xiii... 13	XVI .....xvi 16
II ...ii ... 2	V ...v.... 5	VIII ...viii 8	XI ......xi... 11	XIV ... xiv ...14	XVII ....xvii ... 17
III ..iii ... 3	VI ..vi .. 6	IX ......ix... 9	XII .....xii . 12	XV .... xv 15	XVIII .. xviii .. 18

SOME TERMS AND SIGNS

Here is a list of the most important terms and signs you will find in this book:

:‖   Repeat. Return to the beginning or the nearest ‖:   and play again.

⊓   Pick down. Strike the string by moving your pick down toward the floor.

∨   Pick up. Strike the string by moving your pick up toward the ceiling.

H   Half Step. A distance of one fret on the guitar.

W   Whole step. Equals two half steps. A distance of two frets on the guitar.

♭   Flat. Lower the note one half step (one fret).

♯   Sharp. Raise the note one half step (one fret).

♮   Natural. Cancels a sharp or flat.

Root   The note on which a scale or chord is based.

Ⓡ   Root.

PM   Palm mute.

>   Accent. To place emphasis on a specific note or chord.

⑤   Circled numbers represent strings. ⑤ indicates the 5th string.

✗   Chuck. Mute the strings with the left hand and strum with the right.

⌣   Slur. Used to indicate a hammer-on or a pull-off, and sometimes, a slide.
or ⌣

♩♩   Slide. Pluck the first note. Slide your left hand finger up or down to the second.

BASIC TECHNIQUE

RIGHT HAND

Most players prefer to hold the pick between the thumb and index finger. Place the pick between the flat pad of the thumb and the left side of the index fingertip. Picking is done in either a downward (towards the floor) or upward (towards the ceiling) motion. Keep the right hand relaxed and hold the pick fairly close to its point. Try a medium gauge pick at first, and then move towards a heavy one as your technique improves.

When playing quicker notes, such as eighth notes, we will usually pick down ⊓ on the number counts (downbeats) and up ∨ on the "&" counts (upbeats). This is called *alternate picking*. With sixteenth notes, pick down on the number and "&" counts and up on the "e" and "ah" counts.

Here are some right hand exerices using the E on the open 1st string.

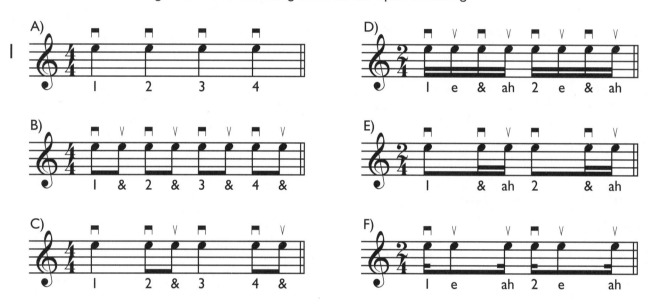

THE LEFT HAND

The proper playing position for the left hand is one which allows you to place all four fingers directly behind the frets. Keep your thumb behind the neck and your wrist low. Do not allow the palm of your left hand to come into contact with the neck. Slightly curl your fingers for maximum leverage and let them do the work, not your hand and arm.

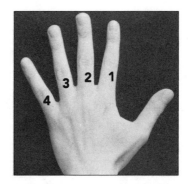

These finger exercises are in the *first position*. In other words, when playing the 1st fret, use your 1st finger, when playing the 2nd fret use your 2nd finger, and so on. Use alternate picking throughout.

Play this sequence twice on each string. Hold your left-hand fingers down until it is absolutley necessary to lift them to play a note on a lower fret.

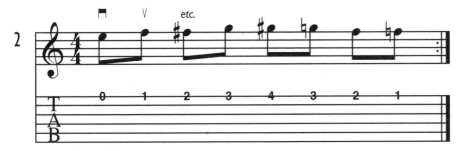

This should also be played twice on each string. The 1st finger should remain down throughout.

This sequence should be played twice on each pair of strings (1st and 2nd, 2nd and 3rd, 3rd and 4th, etc.). Hold down 1 and 3 as 2 and 4 play.

Accidentals remain in force for the entire measure unless they are cancelled by a natural ♮.

Play this sequence up the string for the entire length of the fingerboard and then repeat it on the other five strings. Notice the *slide* lines. To slide, keep your finger on the string as you move to a new fret. We are using the slide technique as a means to *shift* (change positions) up the neck. In Chapter 5 you will learn about slides as an expressive technique.

continue...

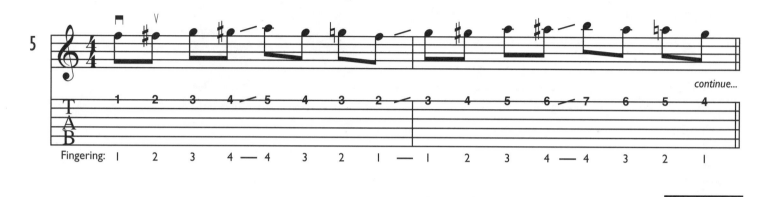

After playing this pattern on all of the strings, repeat it one fret higher, and continue up the neck, one fret at a time.

Jimmy Page
Together with his band, Led Zeppelin, Jimmy Page pioneered the heavy sound that was later called "metal." Page's playing was heavily influenced by the blues.

CHAPTER 2

Rock Theory Review

THE MAJOR SCALE

This material was covered in *Beginning Rock Guitar*. If you have mastered it already, move on to Chapter 3. It is probably a good idea to glance through this chapter just to make sure you are ready to go on. If you have not completed *Beginning Rock Guitar*, study this material carefully.

Any discussion of music theory is based on the *major scale* and how other scales and chords relate to it. The major scale is the familiar "do re mi..." scale. A major scale can be sung or played starting on any note. The first note of the scale, the *root* or *tonic*, gives the scale its name. For instance, a major scale starting on the note C is a C Major scale.

A *scale* is a series of notes arranged in a specific pattern of whole and half steps. The letter names always appear in alphabetical order.

A major scale has seven notes. Here is the formula of whole (W) and half steps (H) for the major scale:

W   W   H   W   W   W   H

Below, this formula is applied to a scale beginning on C. Together, these notes comprise the *key* of C Major. Notice that each note in the scale has a numerical name, as well its letter name. For instance, the note D in a C Major scale is the *2nd scale degree*, or "2."

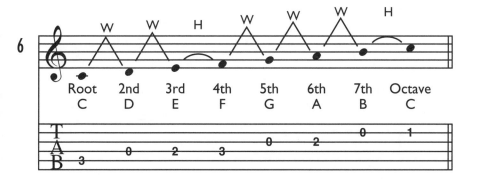

Notice that when the major scale starts on C, the half steps fall naturally between E - F and B - C. No accidentals are required to make the seven notes fit the major scale formula. A major scale built on any root other than C will require either sharps or flats to bring about the correct sequence of whole and half steps.

MAJOR SCALE ON ONE STRING

The major scale pattern is most easily seen on the guitar when played on one string. Start on any note and follow the pattern to build any major scale. Remember: for a half step, go to the next adjacent fret; for whole steps, skip one fret. Name the notes as you play. No letter name can be used more than once (except for the root).

Here is the C Major scale on the 5th string.

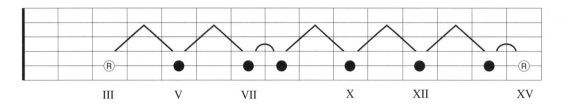

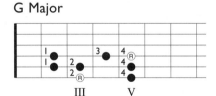

Ⓡ = Root

Remember: This sequence can be played starting on any note on any string.

ONE OCTAVE MAJOR SCALES IN ONE POSITION

A position is a span of four or five adjacent frets. For instance, the 2nd position includes the 2nd, 3rd, 4th, 5th and sometimes 6th or 1st frets. The 1st finger plays the 2nd fret, the 2nd finger plays the 3rd, etc.

Here are four one-octave, one-position fingerings for the major scale.

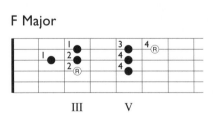

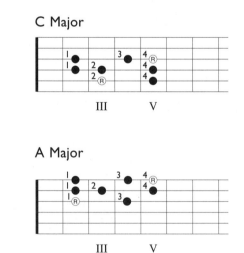

KEY SIGNATURES

The area between the clef and the time signature at the beginning of a piece of music is called the *key signature*. The sharps or flats found in the key signature are derived from the major scale that is the source of all or most of the notes and chords being used. The number of sharps or flats, or their absence, will tell you the key of the piece. In other words, if you see three sharps in the key signature, you know the piece is in the key of A Major, because the A Major scale has three sharps (see the chart below). One flat means the piece is in F Major (see the chart below).

RELATIVE MINOR KEYS

For every major key there is a *relative minor key* which is built on the 6th degree of the major scale. For instance, in the key of C, the note A is the 6th degree (C-D-E-F-G-A), so A Minor is the relative minor key of C Major. The A Minor scale would be as follows: A-B-C-D-E-F-G. The distinguishing feature of a minor scale is the smaller interval between the 1st and 3rd degrees (A and C): it is a whole step plus a half step, instead of two whole steps, as in the major scale.

The chart below shows all the flat and sharp key signatures with their corresponding major and minor keys. The key of C Major (and A Minor), has no sharps or flats.

The *cycle of 5ths* is a very useful musical tool that we can use to learn the key signatures.

Here is how to use the cycle:

The key of C is the natural key (no sharps or flats). As you move clockwise through the cycle you will find the names of the keys that have sharps in their key signatures. Each key is a 5th (3½ steps) up from the previous key. The number indicates the number of sharps in that key. To find the notes that are sharped in each key, start with F♯ in the key of G and add a new sharp for each key. The name of the new sharp is always up a 5th from the previous one.

Moving counterclockwise from C, you will find the names of the keys that have flats in their key signatures. Each name is up a 4th from the previous letter. The number indicates the number of flats in that key. To find the notes that are flatted in each key, start with B♭ in the key of F and add a new flat for each key. The name of the new flat is up a 4th from the previous one.

Remember that when counting a 4th or a 5th, include the two names being compared. For instance, C D E F G, C to G is a 5th.

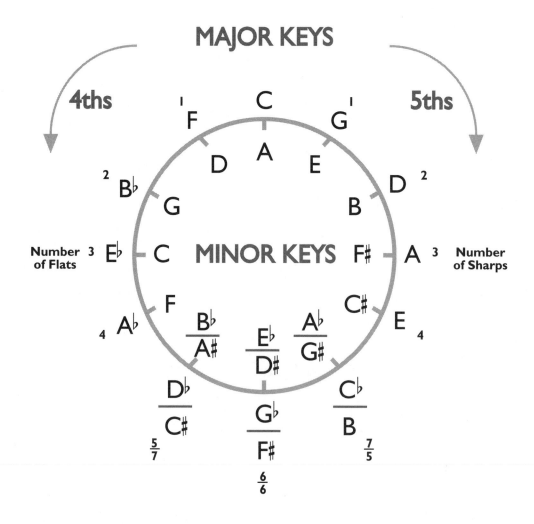

NUMBERING (SPELLING)

Musicians often communicate using *numbering*. In this system, each number refers to a scale degree of the major scale. For instance, in the key of C, the numbers are as follows:

1	2	3	4	5	6	7	1
C	D	E	F	G	A	B	C

Any scale or chord can be given a *formula* or *spelling* by comparing the notes involved to a major scale. For instance, if the scale or chord is built on a C root, and contains an E, the E is called 3. If the scale or chord contains an E♭, the E♭ is called ♭3. G would be 5; G♯, ♯5. Here are two samples:

The formula for an A Major scale is:

1	2	3	4	5	6	7	8
A	B	C♯	D	E	F♯	G♯	A

The formula for an A Minor scale is:

1	2	♭3	4	5	♭6	♭7	8
A	B	C(♮)	D	E	F(♮)	G(♮)	A

Here the basic chord formulas spelled with the note C as the root:

C Major	1	3	5	
	C	E	G	

C Minor	1	♭3	5	
	C	E♭	G	

C Diminished	1	♭3	♭5	
	C	E♭	G♭	

C Augmented	1	3	5♯	
	C	E	G♯	

C Major 7	1	3	5	7
	C	E	G	B

C Dominant 7	1	3	5	♭7
	C	E	G	B♭

THE MINOR PENTATONIC SCALE

The minor pentatonic scale is the most basic and widely used scale for rock soloing. It is a five-note scale. Here is how the spelling for the minor pentatonic scale looks in A:

I	♭3	4	5	♭7
A	C	D	E	G

THE FIVE MINOR PENTATONIC FINGERINGS

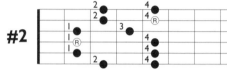

These are the five basic one-position fingerings for this scale. Review them and make sure you know them well before continuing in this book.

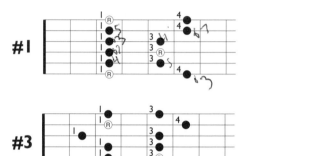

#1

#2

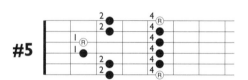

#3

#4

#5

THE ENTIRE MINOR PENTATONIC SYSTEM

Here is how the five fingerings connnect. This diagram shows the scale in the key of A.

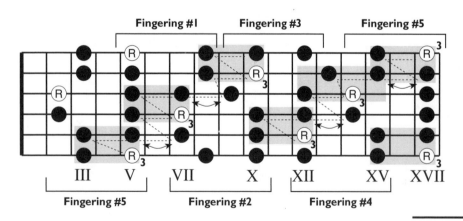

= Slide to new fingering

= Suggestions for connections

(R)₃ = Areas where the 3rd finger plays the root. It is good to think of these areas as being "home base."

THE MAJOR PENTATONIC SCALE

The the major pentatonic is another widely used scale. It is a five-note scale that is used in major keys. Here is how the spelling for the major pentatonic scale looks in A:

1	2	3	5	6
A	B	C#	E	F#

THE FIVE MAJOR PENTATONIC FINGERINGS

These are the five basic one-position fingerings for this scale. Review them and make sure you know them well before continuing in this book.

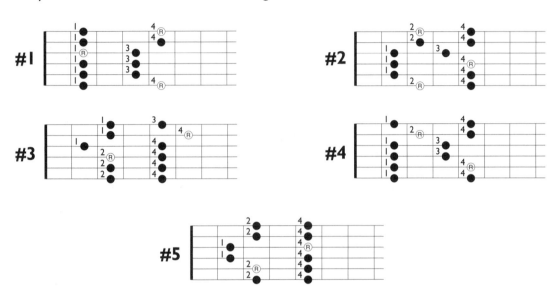

THE ENTIRE MAJOR PENTATONIC SYSTEM

Here is how the five fingerings connnect. This diagram shows the scale in the key of A.

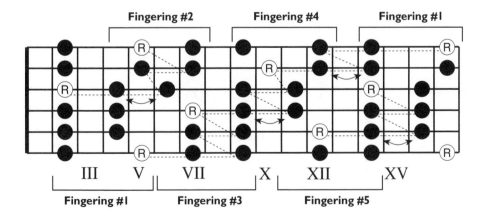

CHAPTER 3

Left-Hand Techniques

Here is a quick review of the left-hand techniques you should know before moving ahead in this book. Make sure these examples are easy for you before proceeding. If you are unfamiliar with any of these techniques, study Chapter 5 of *Beginning Rock Guitar*.

HAMMER-ONS AND PULL-OFFS

Hammer-ons with open strings

Hammer-ons in a higher position on the neck

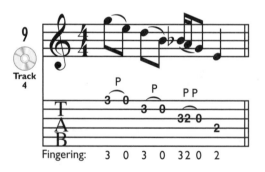

H = Hammer-on

Pull-offs using open strings

Pull-offs in a higher position on the neck

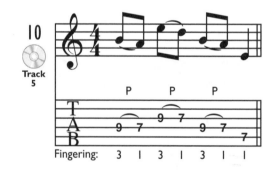

P = Pull-off

SLIDES

s = slide
/ = slide up
\ = slide down

VIBRATO

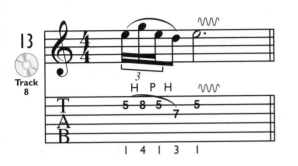

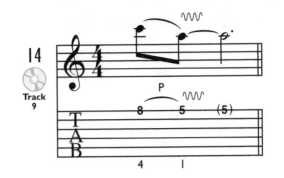

ᔛᔛ = vibrato

BENDING

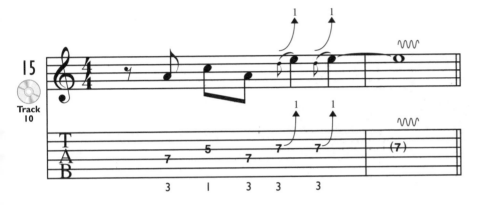

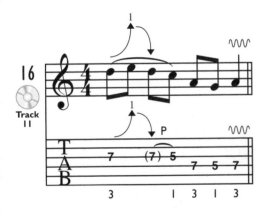

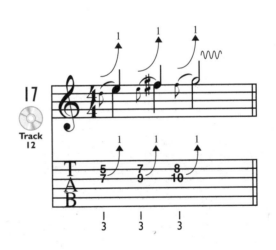

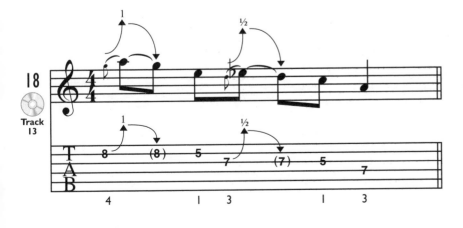

CHAPTER 4

Major Scales

PLAYING TWO-OCTAVE MAJOR SCALES

Learning two-octave major scale fingerings is a very important part of your technical training. These fingerings are also extremely important since they are the basis for all the modal scales and fingerings we will learn later in this book.

Remember, it is the arrangement of whole and half steps that give the major scale its specific sound and characteristics. Keeping the formula in mind (see page 17) will help you learn these fingerings.

The first two-octave major scale fingering we will look at begins with the 2nd finger playing the tonic on the 6th string. Here it is in G:

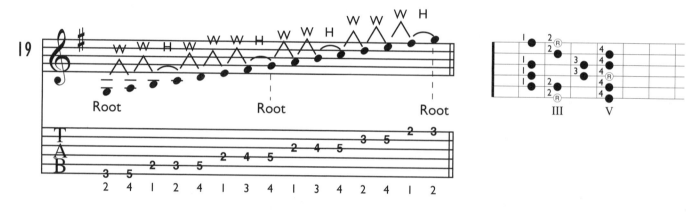

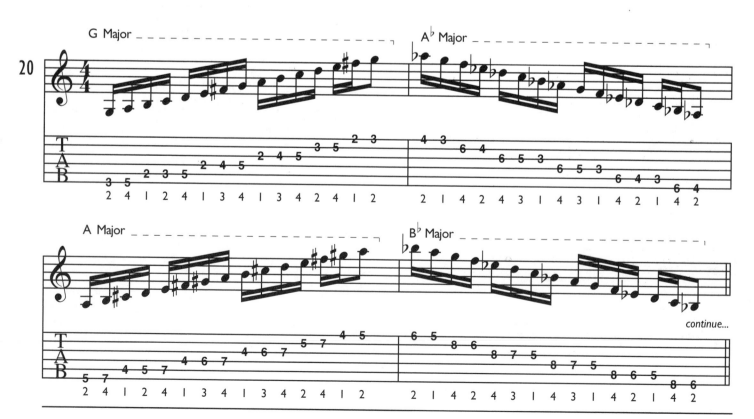

continue...

This two-ocatve major scale fingering begins with the 4th finger playing the tonic on the 6th string.

21

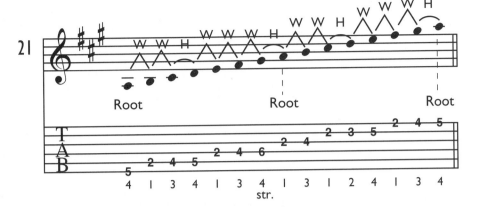

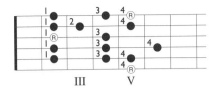

str. =	Stretch the finger without moving the enitre hand.	

Here's one that begins with the 1st finger playing the tonic on the 6th string.

22

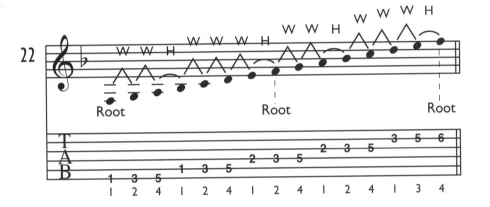

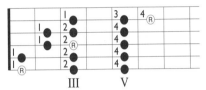

Todd Mohr
Leader of Big Head Todd and the Monsters, Todd Mohr is know for his infectious grooves.

MELODIC PATTERNS

Once you have the scale patterns under your fingers, you can begin to develop *melodic patterns* using the scale tones. Melodic patterns are groups of two or more notes in a specific shape that can be generated from every scale degree. Usually, they are *motives* (short distinctive musical ideas) using the scale notes in a particular pattern that are then *sequenced* (repeated on different pitches). For instance, in a 1-2-3-1 pattern, we play the 1st, 2nd, 3rd and then the 1st notes of the scale. Then, we proceed to sequence this pattern through the scale (2-3-4-2, 3-4-5-3, etc.) Here are some melodic patterns using the G Major scale.

25

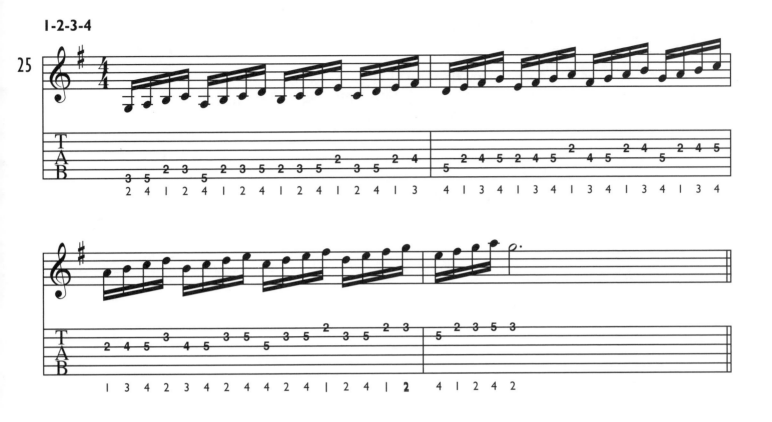

26

You can use these melodic patterns to practice every new scale you learn. There are lots of other possibilities, some of which will be demonstrated later in this book. Each time a new scale is introduced, different melodic patterns will be given. But you can use any melodic pattern for any scale! Experiment. Make up your own. Have fun!

LICKS USING THE MAJOR SCALE

Major scale licks have a very specific sound. Some of the licks below will remind you of players that often use the major sound, such as Duane Allman of the Allman Brothers Band. Create more licks of your own using the major scale.

A la Jerry Garcia

A la Dickie Betts

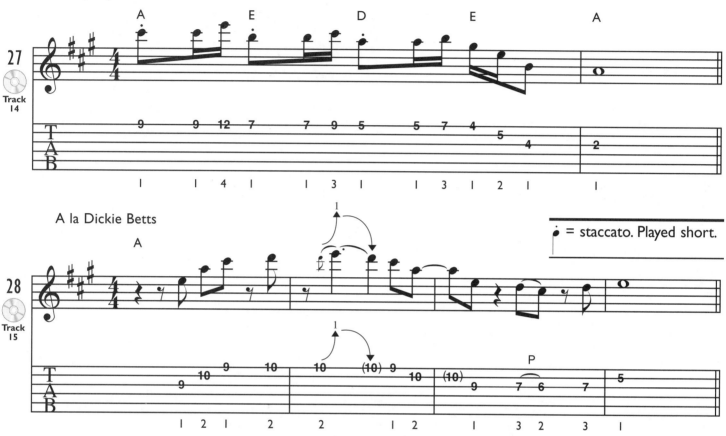

A la Billy Corgan. The "x" symbols represent *chucks* (mute the strings with the left hand as you strum).

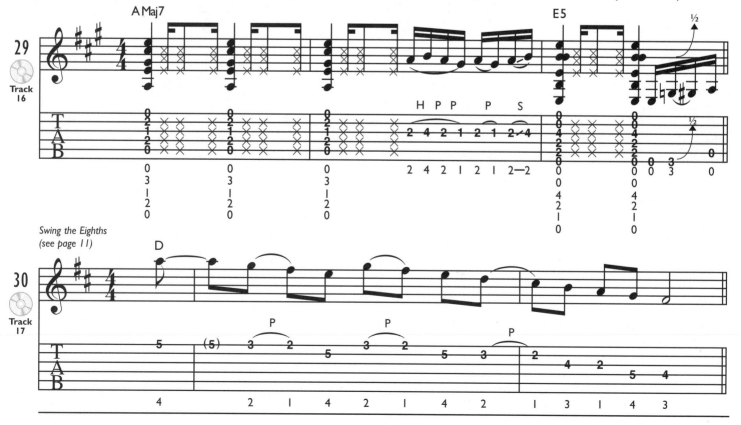

The major scale will work well over progressions that use the *diatonic chords* of the major scale. In other words, if all the chords in a progression are formed from the notes of a single major scale, you can use that major scale to improvise over that progression.

Use the melodic patterns and scale fingerings you have learned as building blocks for your solos. Try to invent short melodies and riffs and develop them. Be creative.

All four of the following chord progresssions use diatonic chords of the major scale. As you learned in *Beginning Rock Guitar*, Chapter 6, Roman numerals are used to indicate the scale degeee on which a chord is built—upper case for major or dominant chords and lower case for minor or diminished. For instance, the 2nd scale degreee in the key of G is A, and diatonic chords built on the 2nd degree are always minor, so it is marked "ii."

Use the G Major scale.

Use the A Major scale.

Use the E Major scale.

Use the D Major scale.

FINGERINGS WITH THREE NOTES PER STRING

Playing three notes per string is one of the most common ways to finger scales of all kinds in modern rock playing. A great way to generate these fingerings for the major scale is to start from each successive note of the scale on the 6th string and play through the scale using three notes per string.

The seven diagrams that follow are all the F Major scale. Each one starts on a different note of the scale: the first one starts on F, the next on G, the next on A, etc. As you go through these, you will notice that the fingerings lend themselves well to playing triplets.

THE F MAJOR SCALE

(●) = Alternative fingerings for playing in one position.

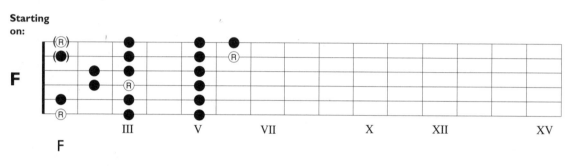

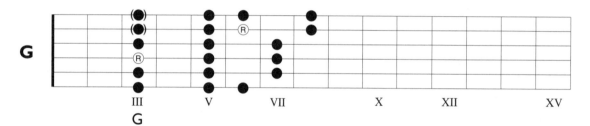

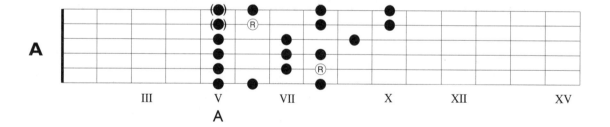

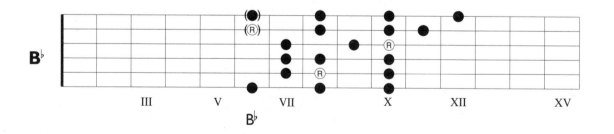

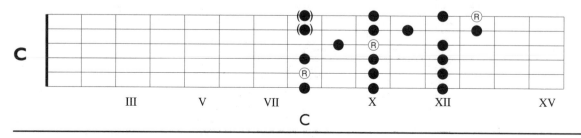

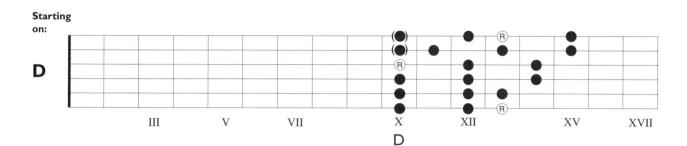

D

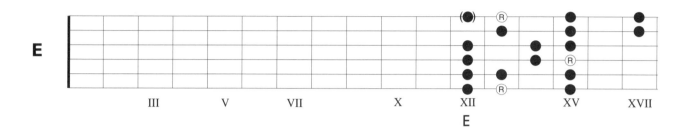

E

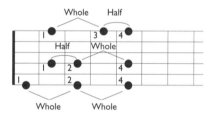

Throughout this book, starting with the F Major scale fingerings above, you will encounter "three-note-per-string" fingerings. When fingering scales in this manner, there are three usual combinations of notes on any given string, as shown in the list on the right:

This diagam shows the best fingers to use for each of these combinations.

whole step - half step
half step - whole step
whole step - whole step

Joe Satriani
One of the most successful rock instrumentalists, Satriani is known for his extreme style and technique.

CHAPTER 5

Intervals

The distance between any two notes, whether they are in a scale, chord or melody, is called an *interval*. Understanding intervals is important for grasping many of the theoretical concepts you will encounter as you advance as a musician. Furthermore, certain intervals are very useful in lead and rhythm guitar playing. This chapter will help get you started understanding and using intervals.

INTERVAL NAMES

Every interval name has two parts: a size name (a number, such as 3rd, 4th or 6th) and a quality name (such as major, minor or perfect).

SIZE
The basic intervals, sometimes called simple intervals, fall within the span of an octave (a distance of twelve half steps):

2nd, 3rd, 4th, 5th 6th, 7th, octave

Larger intervals, called *extensions* or *compound intervals*, are bigger:

9th, 11th, 13th

QUALITY
Here are the quality names and their abbreviations:

<u>Name</u>	<u>Abreviation</u>
Major	Maj
Minor	min
Augmented	Aug
Diminished	dim
Perfect	P

The chart in Example 35 shows the simple intervals measured up from the note C.

You will notice that the augmented 4th and diminished 5th fall on the same frets, and therefore sound the same. That is because they are *enharmonically equivalent* (see page 7). Also, you should study Example 35 and make the following observations:

- The size of an interval is determined by the number of letter names between the two notes, including the two notes. For example, C to A is a 6th (C_1 - D_2 - E_3 - F_4 - G_5 - A_6).
- The minor intervals are one half step smaller than the major intervals. So, you can make a major interval minor by lowering the upper note with an accidental, thus decreasing the distance between the two notes.
- The diminished intervals are one half step smaller than the perfect intervals. So, you can make a perfect interval diminished by lowering the upper note with an accidental, thus decreasing the distance between the two notes.
- The augmented intervals are one half step larger than the perfect and major intervals. So, you can make a perfect or major interval augmented by raising the upper note with an accidental, thus increasing the distance between the two notes.

INTERVALS SHAPES

Below are some useful interval shapes for you to learn.

For any pair of strings except the 2nd and 3rd strings:

Maj3   min3   P4   P5

The following shapes only work on the 2nd and 3rd strings:

Maj3   min3   P4   P5

The following shapes are on the 4th and 2nd strings, but work for the 3rd and 1st strings, too.

Maj6   min6

The following shapes are on the 5th and 3rd strings, but work for the 6th and 4th strings, too.

Maj6   min6

HARMONIZATION — 3RDS, 6THS, 4THS AND 5THS

Harmony is the result produced when two or more notes are sounded together. Using major and minor 3rds is a very common way to harmonize a line. The 3rds have a sweet, vocal quality. The 6th spreads the harmony out for a fuller sound, and they fit particularly well on the guitar fingerboard. Perfect 4ths and 5ths have a more open, undefined sound and are often used for harmony in two-guitar situations.

Since 6ths are played on two nonadjacent strings with one unplayed string in between, you will have to use the left hand finger that plays the lower note to deaden the inside string.

Several of the examples below are in the *Mixolydian mode*. A mode is a reordering of a scale. The Mixolydian mode is simply the notes of the major scale played starting and ending on the 5th degree. For instance, the 5th degree of a D Major scale is A, so if you play a D Major scale starting and ending on A, you have played the A Mixolydian mode. See page 75 for a more detailed explanation.

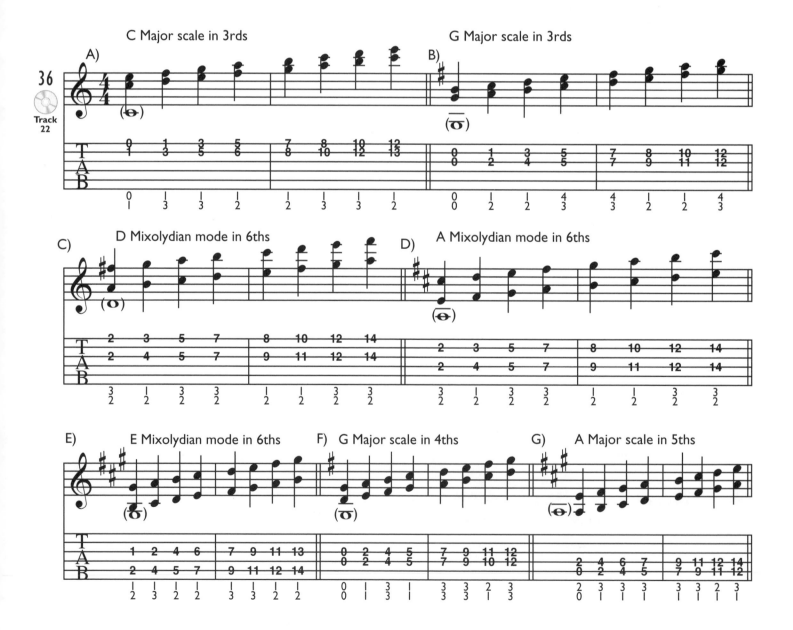

Here are some examples of harmonization with intervals:

A blues riff using 6ths in the style of Eric Clapton. Swing the eighths (see page 11).

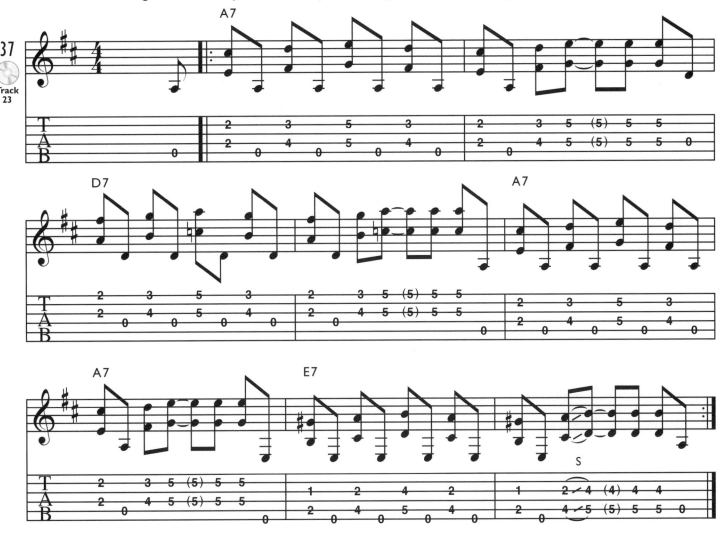

A riff using 5ths in the style of Bob Marley or Fleetwood Mac.

The same riff as Example 38 using 4ths.

CHAPTER 6

Triads

Chords are harmonious groups of notes taken from a particular scale. The *voicings* (arrangements of tones within a chord) we have learned up to now have been either open or movable forms using four, five or six notes (doubling some of the notes of the chord). It is also important to learn *close* voicings which use only the three basic chord tones within one octave. We call these voicings *triads*. This is another use of the same term used to describe the strictly theoretical concept of a three-note chord built in 3rds. Triads can be played on any adjacent group of three strings. In this chapter, we will look at major and minor triads. Here is a quick review of their formulas:

Major	I	3	5
Minor	I	♭3	5

As you learned in *Beginning Rock Guitar*, every triad can appear in *root position* (with the root as the lowest note, or in *inversion* (with a note other than the root in the lowest position). There are two possible inversions. When played as triads on adjacent strings, the voicings for the inversions look like this:

Root Position	I	3	5
1st Inversion	3	5	I
2nd Inversion	5	I	3

As you will see from the following examples, guitar players use triads in diverse ways, both for rhythm and lead playing. Triads can also be broken down into *diads* (double stops or two-note chords) and can be *embellished* (ornamented) with related scale notes and riffs in each position.

PHOTO • RANDI ANGLIN PHOTOGRAPHY

Begin by learning the sequence of inversions for major and minor triads up and down any three-string group by reading across the following chart. The three-string group of strings 2, 3 and 4 is probably the most valuable. Next, try reading down the chart to learn how to move across the string sets through the inversions. Once you have mastered that, begin using triads to play chord progressions. When choosing your inversions, try to avoid large position leaps. This will result in better voice leading and a more pleasing sound (see page 41).

Dave Matthews
Innovative musician and leader of the Dave Matthews Band, he is known for his funky rhythmic grooves.

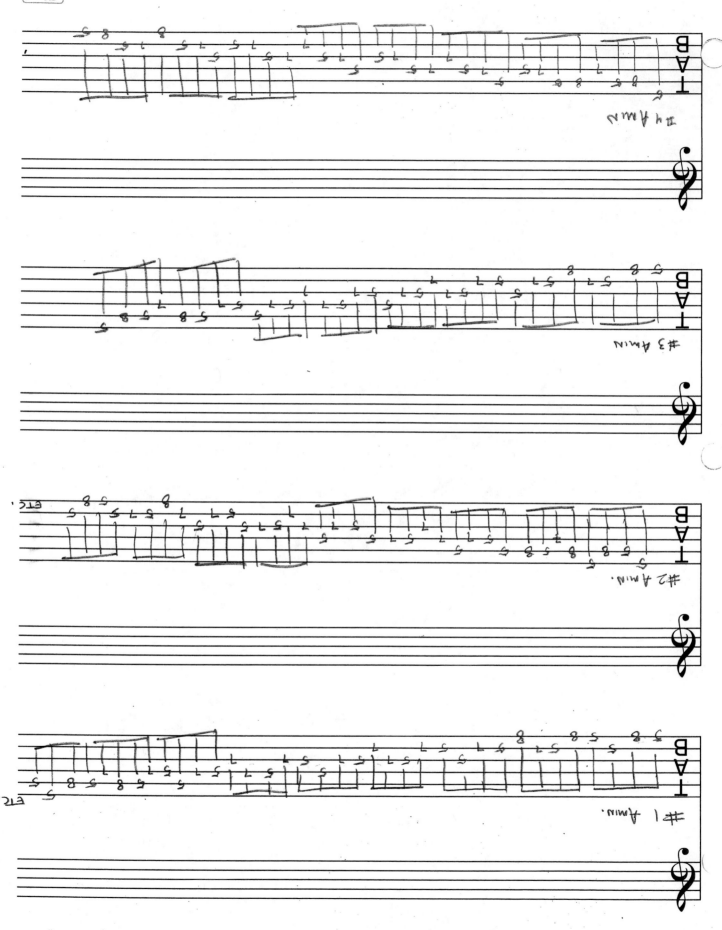

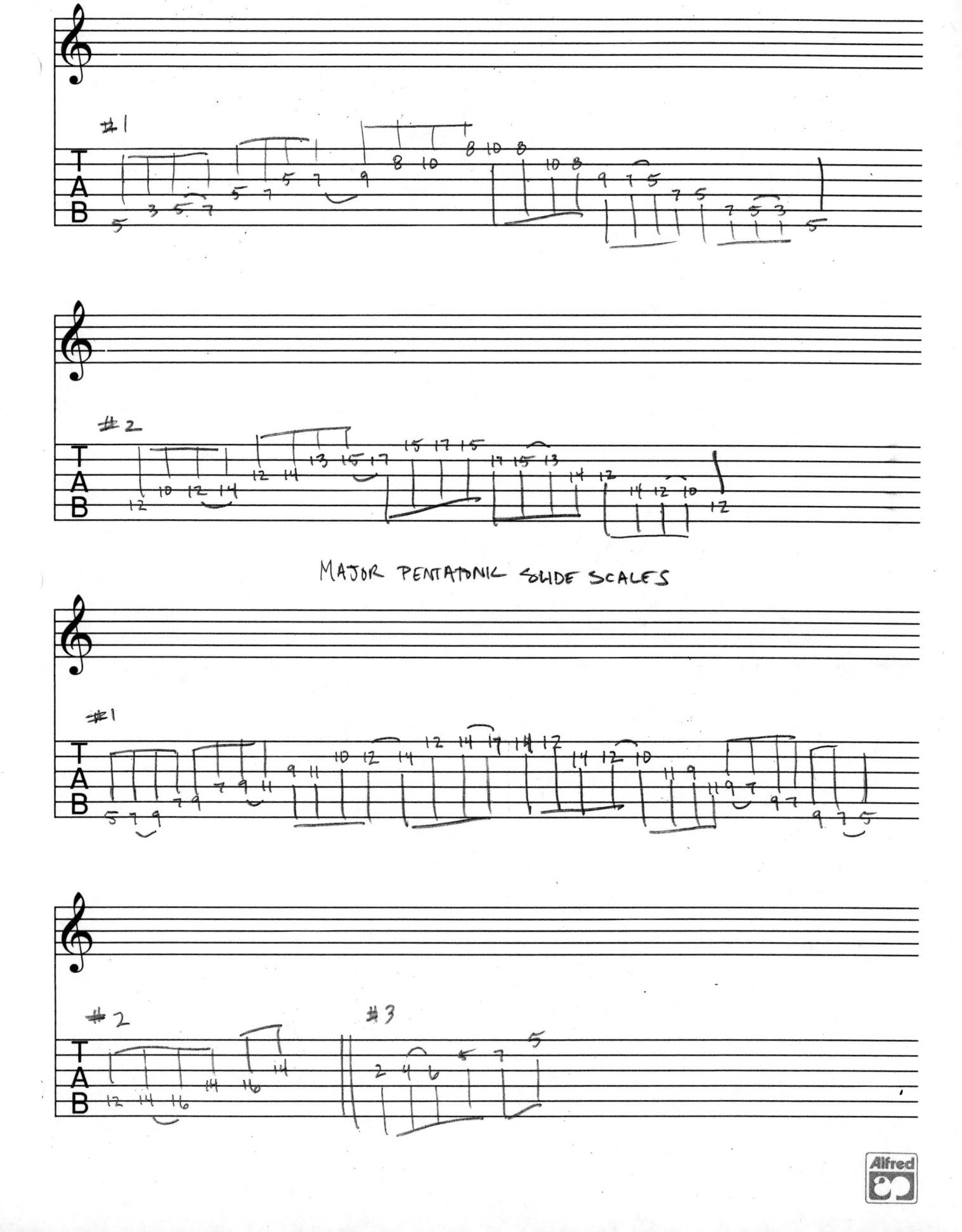

The chords in the following charts all have B♭ as the root, because this key very clearly demonstrates how the triads relate on the fingerboard. Try to find major and minor pentatonic scale fingerings that are close in position to each triad. This will make them even more useful to you. First, read the charts from left to right. Then read down each column.

MAJOR TRIADS (in B♭)

Three-String Groups

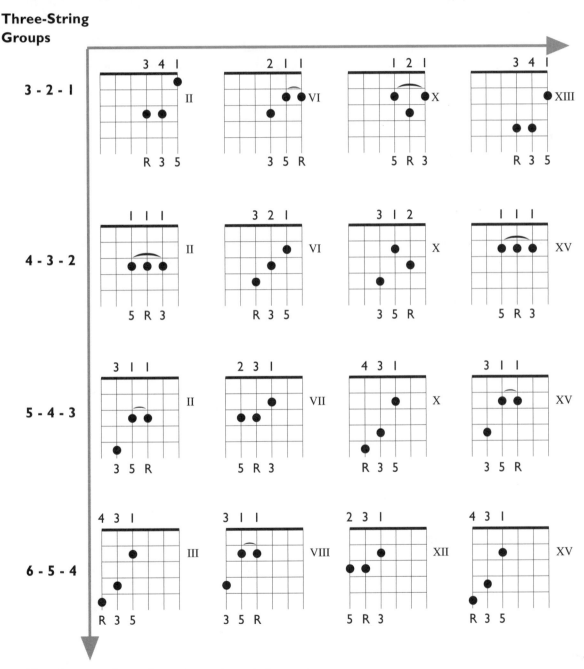

This diagram shows how the major triads overlap.

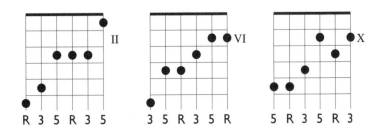

Three-String Groups

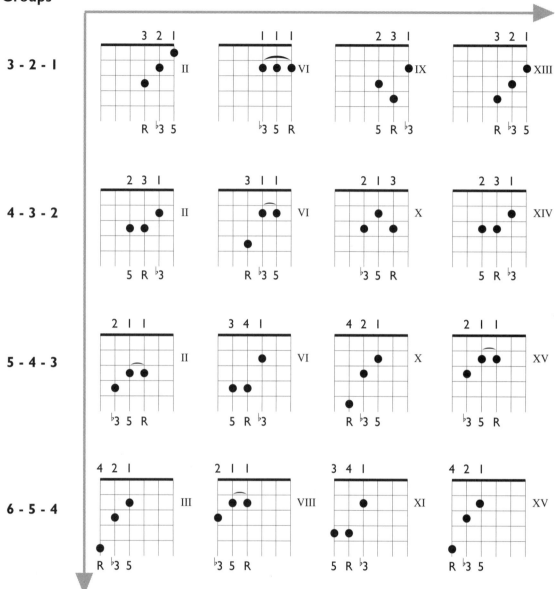

This diagram shows how the minor triads overlap.

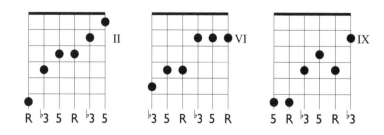

VOICE LEADING

Voice leading is the way each note (*voice*) of a chord moves when changing from one chord to another. Listen to how each voice moves in a melodic way as you change between two chords. There are times when a voice might not change at all. These are called *common tones.*

To see how this works, play the examples below. They show the I, IV, V and I chords in the key of D Major using triads. As you read from left to right you will notice that there is as little movement as possible between chords. Notice the use of common tones. This is a more practical way to change chords than moving the same inversion all over the neck. By using different inversions for each chord, your voice leading will be much smoother. Try this in other keys.

Read across from left to right.

Three-string Group 4 - 3 - 2

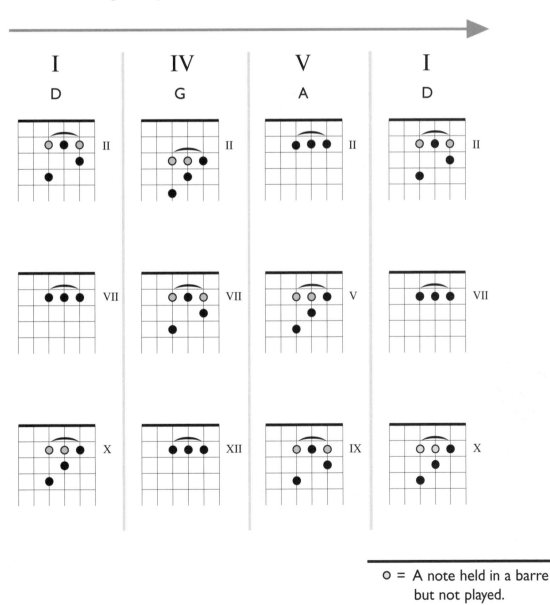

○ = A note held in a barre
but not played.

Three-string Group 3 - 2 - 1

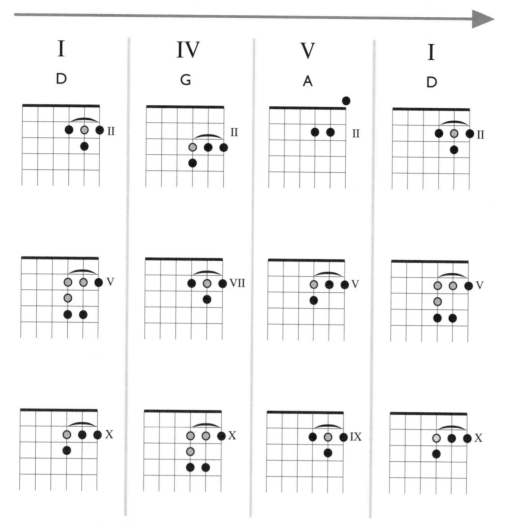

| I | IV | V | I |
| D | G | A | D |

*Jimi Hendrix
Hendrix raised triad
playing to a high art.*

in the style of Randy Rhodes

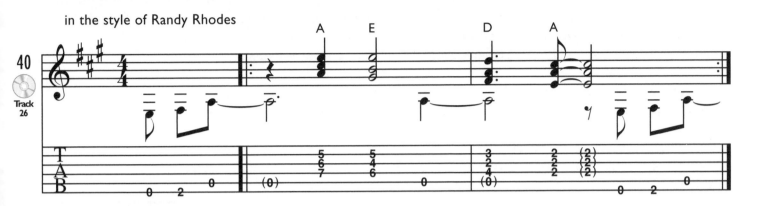

in the style of The Black Crowes

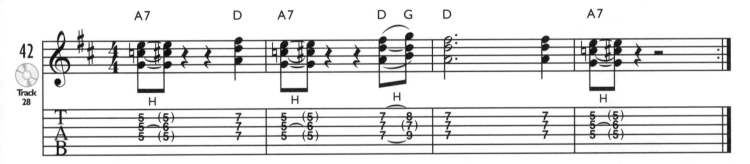

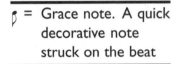 = Grace note. A quick decorative note struck on the beat

in the style of Joe Walsh

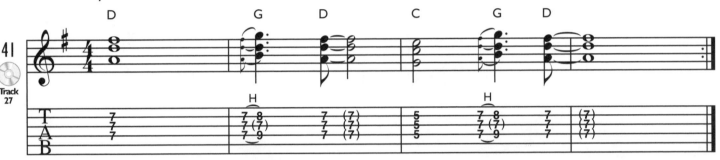

in the style of Keith Richards

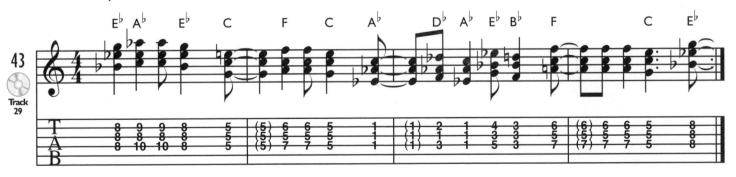

CHORD EMBELLISHMENTS

The triads you have learned, and other larger chords that you know, can be embellished with scale tones and licks. Jimi Hendrix was a master of this essential guitar skill. Eddie Van Halen, Joe Satriani, Jeff Beck and Keith Richards also make great music with this technique.

The following pages show some of the most common examples of this style. Notice that, usually, one note of a chord will sustain as another is embellished.

This diagram shows notes that can be added around a G triad on the string group of 1, 2 and 3 as embellishments. The arrows illustrate how you can move to and from the embellishments.

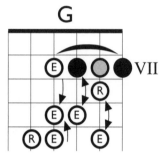

® =	Root
Ⓔ =	Embellishment
○ =	A note held in a barre but not played

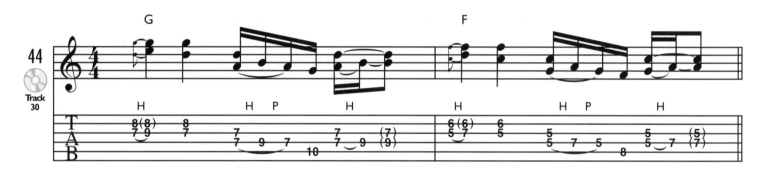

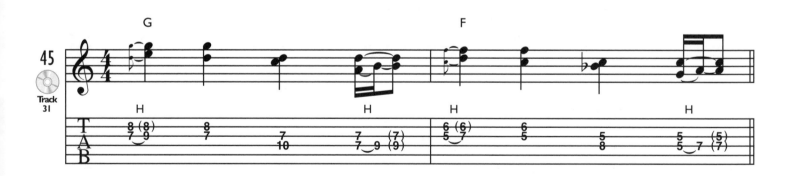

Here are the embellishments for a D triad on the 4, 3, 2 string group.

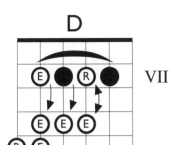

Here are the embellishments for an A triad on the 3, 2, 1 string group.

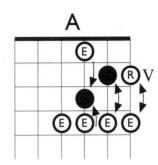

Example 46A and 46B use the embellished D triad. Examples 46C and 46D use the embellished A triad.

CHAPTER 7

Diatonic Harmony

When we build a chord on each note of a major scale using only scale tones we create a system called *diatonic harmony*. The scale tones, and the harmonies they create, comprise the *key* of the root note of the scale. For instance, the notes of a C Major scale comprise the key of C Major. *Diatonic* means "belonging to the key."

Each chord is made by stacking scale tones in 3rds to create triads. Because of the pattern of whole steps and half steps in the major scale, there is a pattern of chord types in diatonic harmony. Let's start by building a C Major scale, and numbering each scale degree for reference..

C Major scale

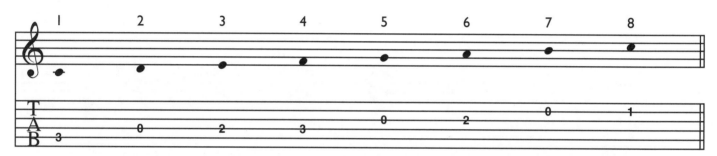

Now, build a triad on C, the 1st scale degree. The result is a C Major triad. A major triad has a major 3rd (a distance of two whole steps) on the bottom and a minor 3rd (a distance of one whole step plus one half step) on the top; C to E is a major 3rd, and E to G is a minor 3rd. Build a triad on D, the 2nd scale degree. The result is a D Minor triad. A minor triad has a minor 3rd on the bottom and a major 3rd on top; D to F is a minor 3rd, and F to A is a major 3rd. All the diatonic triads in a major keys are major or minor, except for the one built on the 7th scale degree, which is diminished. A diminished triad has a minor 3rd on the bottom and a minor 3rd on top.

Here are the diatonic triads of the C major scale. Notice that the harmonies are labeled with Roman numerals (see page 12). Upper case Roman numerals are used to label major triads, and lower case are used to label minor and diminished triads.

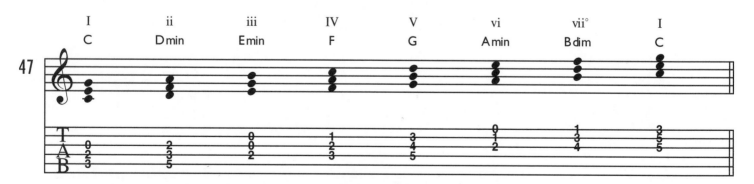

> **To sumarize, in any major key: I, IV and V will always be major;**
> **ii, iii and vi will always be minor; and**
> **vii will always be diminished.**

DIATONIC TRIADS

ROOT POSITION TRIADS IN G MAJOR

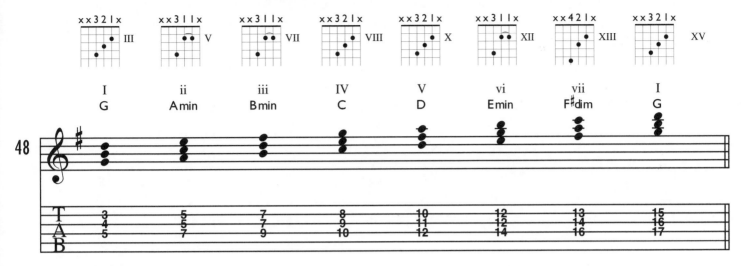

1ST INVERSION TRIADS IN C MAJOR

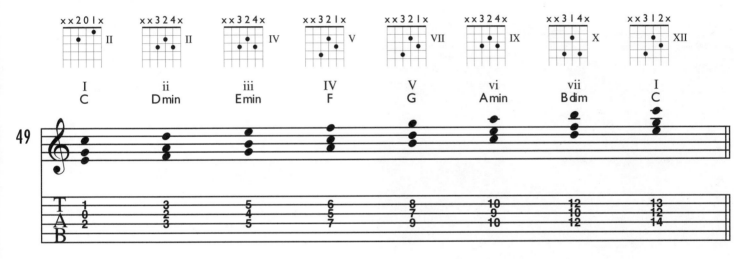

2ND INVERSION TRIADS IN A MAJOR

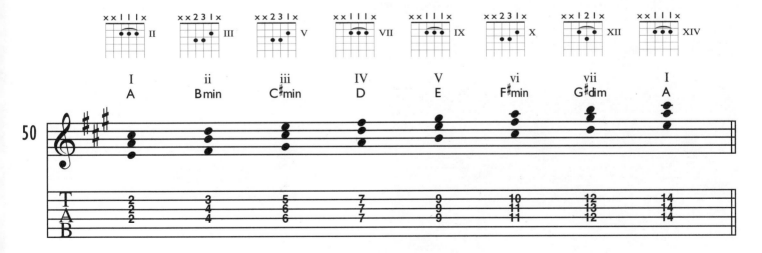

DIATONIC ARPEGGIOS

An *arpeggio* is when the notes of a chord are played one after the other, either ascending or descending. Arpeggios are sometimes refferred to as "broken chords." Read the arpeggios that follow by starting on the 6th string on the lowest note indicated. Then play up each string, moving from the lowest string to the highest, and then back again. They all begin on the root and ascend. You will notice familiar triad shapes in each arpeggio.

DIATONIC ARPEGGIOS IN A MAJOR WITH THE ROOT ON THE 6TH STRING

51

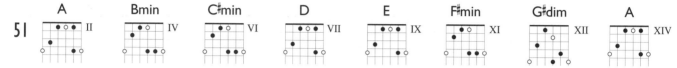

DIATONIC ARPEGGIOS IN D MAJOR WITH THE ROOT ON THE 5TH STRING

52

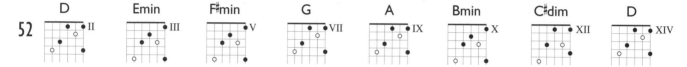

o = Root

Stone Gossard
Stone Gossard's band, Pearl Jam, pioneered the alternative rock movement.

7TH CHORDS

A 7th chord is created by stacking an additional 3rd on top of a basic triad to create a four-note chord. The four types of 7th chords found in major keys are covered in the table below.

CHORD TYPE	SYMBOL	SPELLING			
Major 7th	Maj7	1	3	5	7
Dominant 7th	7	1	3	5	$\flat$7
Minor 7th	min7	1	$\flat$3	5	$\flat$7
Minor 7 flat 5	min7$\flat$5	1	$\flat$3	$\flat$5	$\flat$7

Here are some common fingerings for these important chords:

7th chords with the root on the 6th string.

53

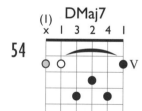 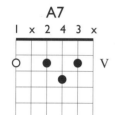 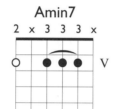 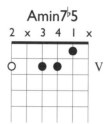

7th chords with the root on the 5th string.

54

 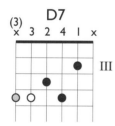 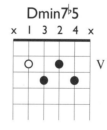 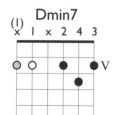

7th chords with the root on the 4th string.

55

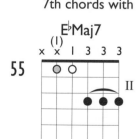 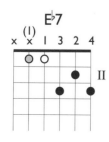 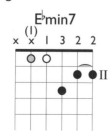 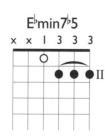

DIATONIC 7TH CHORDS

When we expand our diatonic triads to include an additional 3rd, we create 7th chords on each scale degree. The table below shows the type of 7th chords that will occur on each scale degree in a major key.

> I, IV .... major 7 (Maj7)
> V .... dominant 7 (7)
> ii, iii, vi..... minor 7 (min7)
> vii.............. minor 7 flat 5 (min7♭5)

Here is the pattern of diatonic chord types in major keys:

	I	ii	iii	IV	V	vi	vii
Triads	major	minor	minor	major	major	minor	diminished
7ths	Maj7	min7	min7	Maj7	7	min7	min7♭5

Knowing the notes of any scale allows you to construct the diatonic chords of that key. Try building the diatonic chords of keys that you know, as in Examples 56 and 57. Read across from left to right.

DIATONIC 7TH CHORDS IN G MAJOR

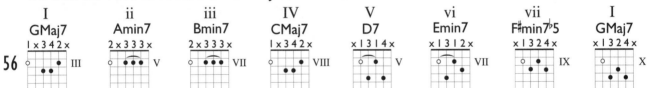

DIATONIC 7TH CHORDS IN C MAJOR

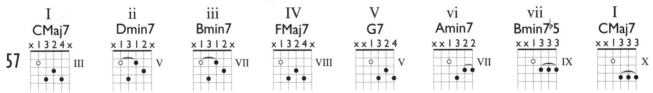

Try using the chord forms shown here, and what you have learned about the chord types, to find new ways of playing songs that you know. Experiment with different variations. Learn some jazz songs ("standards"), most of which make abundant use of 7th chords.

TRANSPOSING

Knowing scales, keys and diatonic chords will make *transposing* (changing keys) a simple matter. The discussion that follows will begin with a chord progression in the key of G Major. Then, you will learn the thought process for transposing it to the key of E Major.

To transpose the progression in Example 58 to the key of E Major, use the following procedure:

Write down the numbers 1 through 7. These represent the scale degrees.
Below the numbers, write the scale notes for the original key (in this case, G Major).
Below that, write the scale notes for the new key (in this case, E Major).

Scale Degrees	1	2	3	4	5	6	7
Key of G Major	G	A	B	C	D	E	F♯
Key of E Major	E	F♯	G♯	A	B	C♯	D♯

To transpose the chord progression in Example 58 from G Major to E Major, simply use the chart above to substitute the appropriate chord. Keep chord qualities the same (for instance, minor chords remain minor, 7th chords remain 7th chords, etc.). So, for example, if the chord was D7 in the original key, play a B7 in the new key because, in your chart, B is under D.

Note that in the original progression, there is an F Major chord, which is not diatonic (natural) to the key of G Major. It still acts as the seventh chord in the key, but it is one half step lower than the usual vii chord. In order to adjust for this when transposing, lower the vii chord by one half step in the new key, and use a D♮ instead of D♯.

Here is the same progression as Example 58, transposed to the key of E Major:

Another way to think about transposition is to rely on the Roman numerals. For instance, transpose the V chord in one key to another key by playing the V chord of the new key. Here are four common chord progressions in G represented by Roman numerals. Try transposing them to other keys.

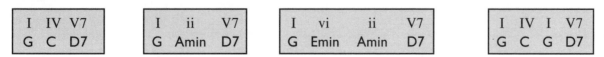

Try your hand at transposing chord progressions that you know, and playing the results.

CHAPTER 8

The Composite Scale

A *composite scale* is made by combining two different types of scales into one. Because of the influence of the blues on rock music, our note choices when improvising in a major key are often drawn from both the major and minor (blues) pentatonic scales. Most players do not limit themselves to a strictly minor or major approach when soloing in a major key. Rather, they will lean more toward one scale and use tones from the other as *passing tones*. Passing tones are non-scale or non-chord tones used to connect scale or chord tones. They are usually short in duration and occur off the beat (on the "&").

Combining the major pentatonic and blues scales (including the ♭5) will result in a common composite scale. Examples 60 and 61 show parallel (starting on the same root) major pentatonic and blues scales in A. Example 62 shows the composite scale that results from combining them.

A MAJOR PENTATONIC SCALE

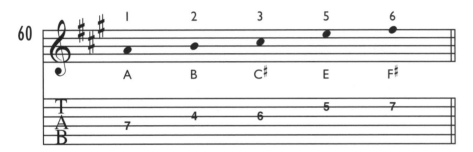

A BLUES SCALE

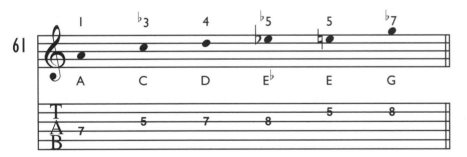

COMPOSITE SCALE IN A

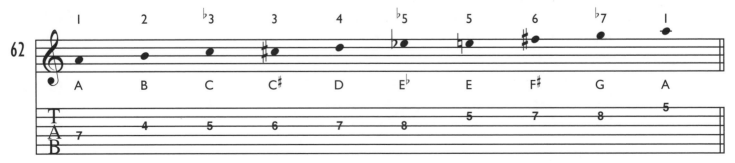

Since you have more note choices when using this scale, you must procede a little more carefully than you would in a strictly pentatonic approach. You will find that as the chords you are playing over change, the appropriate note choices from this scale will change also. For instance, when landing on the major I chord, you will probably avoid the ♭3 from the blues scale and use the 3 from major pentatonic instead. Composites scale such as this are usually used over major and dominant 7th chords.

A composite scale can be found surrounding any of the three major triad positions (root, 1st inversion and 2nd inversion). It is extremely useful to learn the scale as it relates to each of these triad positions.

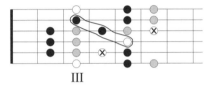

THE COMPOSITE SCALE IN G SURROUNDING THE ROOT POSITION TRIAD

The triad is circled.

○ = Root	
⊗ = ♭5	
◉ = minor pentatonic	
● = major pentatonic	

Here are two licks in G using the composite scale in this configuration. Swing the eighths in both. Notice that the scale degrees are labeled above the music.

THE COMPOSITE SCALE IN G SURROUNDING THE 1ST INVERSION TRIAD

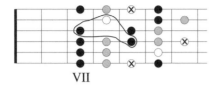

VII

Here are the same two licks again, but this time shown in the new configuration, surrounding the 1st inversion triad. Remember to swing the eighths.

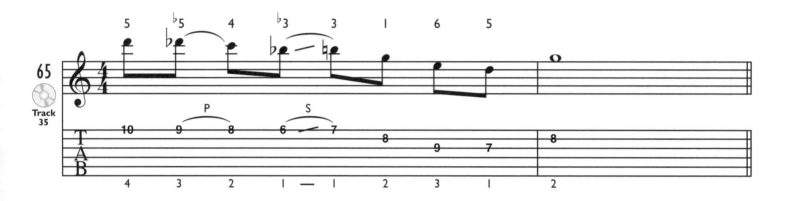

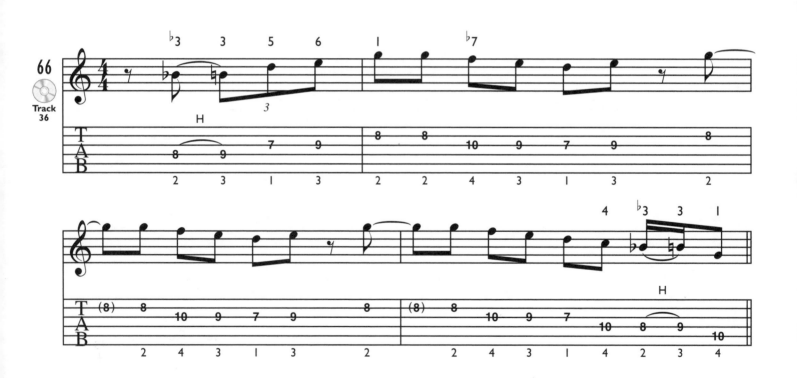

THE COMPOSITE SCALE IN G SURROUNDING THE 2ND INVERSION TRIAD

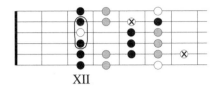

XII

Here they are once again, this time shown in the last configuration, surrounding the 2nd inversion triad. Kepp swinging the eighths.

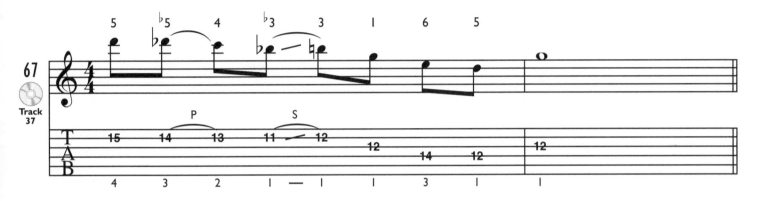

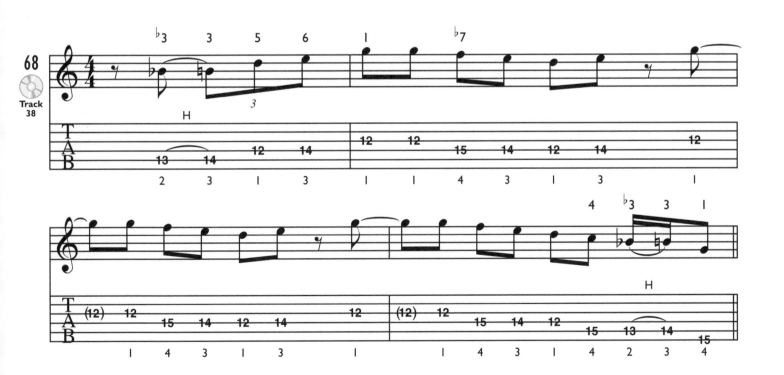

MORE COMPOSITE SCALE LICKS

USING A COMPOSITE SCALE IN A

In the style of Lynyrd Skynyard. Swing those eighths!

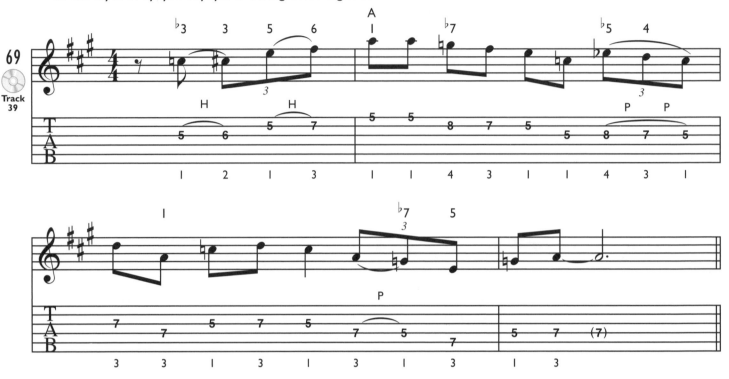

USING A COMPOSITE SCALE IN G

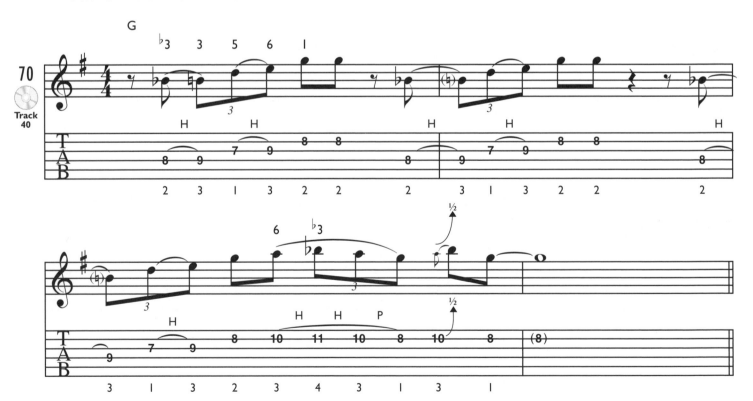

USING A COMPOSITE SCALE IN C. Swing the eighths.

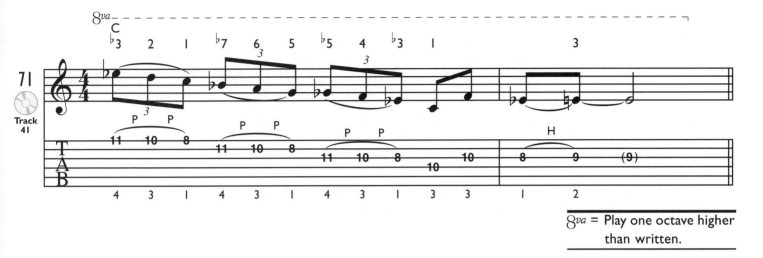

8va = Play one octave higher
than written.

USING A COMPOSITE SCALE IN A. Swing the eighths.

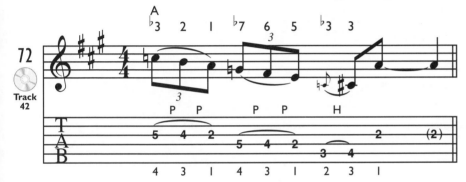

USING A COMPOSITE SCALE IN D. Straight eighths. A la Guns and Roses.

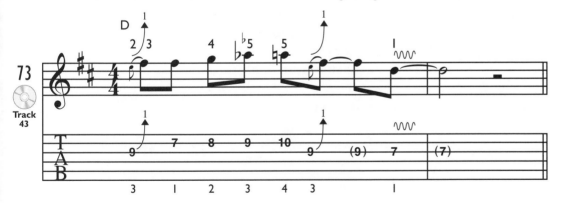

CHAPTER 9

New Chord Forms & Rhythm Guitar

As your technique and understanding of the guitar increases, you will want to find new sounds that will add interest to your playing. One way to do this is to learn *extended* and *altered* chords that introduce new tone colors to the chords you already know. An extended chord is one that stacks additional 3rds on top of a 7th chord (9ths, 11ths or 13ths). An altered chord is one where the 5th or the 9th has been raised or lowered. These chords can be used to add interest to a rhythm guitar part. Many sounds can be created by adding extensions to the chords you know. Doing this will open your ears to hearing new note choices in your solo playing. To fully appreciate the value of the new chords that you will be learning, you first need a foundation in *functional harmony*.

FUNCTIONAL HARMONY

Functional harmony is the study of how chords act in a chord progression. The harmonic movement of a piece of music is dependent upon its chord progression. The most basic movement is between a resolved or static sound to an unresolved or tension sound, as in moving from the I chord of a key (resolved) to the V7 chord (tension) and back again (resolved). This movement between tension and resolution is basic to all styles of music and can be accomplished in simple or complex ways. Try playing back and forth between the I and V7 chords of any key. Notice how strongly your ear wants to hear the I chord end or resolve the sequence.

All chords in a diatonic progression can be grouped into three functional categories. In fact, very often the chords within each category can be substituted for one another without changing the role or function of the given chord. The three functions are: *tonic* (I, resolved): *subdominant* (IV, slight tension) and *dominant* (V, strong tension). Example 74 shows how the diatonic chords are distributed among the three categories. The dotted lines illustrate that the chords of each category contain common tones, making them similar. For instance, E Minor has the notes E and G in common with C Major, and A minor has C and E in common with C Major. So, either E Minor or A Minor could be substituted for I in a chord progression, and still fulfill the tonic function.

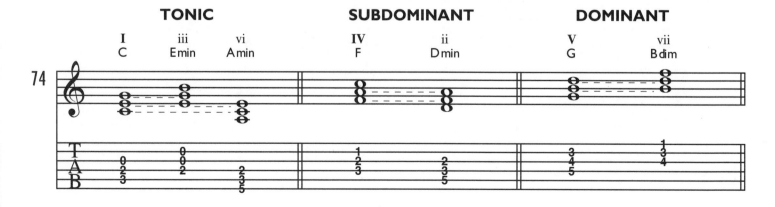

The diminished 7th chord ($1\ \flat3\ \flat5\ \flat\flat7$*) is used as a connector between diatonic chords and as a substitute for dominant function chords. The diminished 7th chord (dim7) is made up entirely of minor 3rds. For instance, if you stack an additional minor 3rd on top of the vii chord in the key of C (Bdim: B-D-F) you get a Bdim7 chord: B-D-F-A$^\flat$.

The following diagrams show three ways of playing diminished 7th chords. The first two forms are usually used as connectors with Root ⑥ and Root ⑤ chords (chords with their roots on the 6th and 5th strings) respectively, while the third form is a higher voicing utilizing only the first four strings.

DIMINSHED 7TH CHORDS

Use to connect
Root ⑥ chords

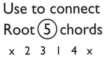

Use to connect
Root ⑤ chords

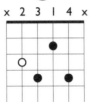

Use to connect chords
with the root on any string

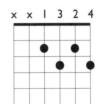

* The double flat sign ($\flat\flat$) indicates that the pitch should be lowered a whole step.

Examples 75 and 76 show how diminished 7th chords can be used to connect diatonic chords.

ROOT ⑥ CHORDS IN G

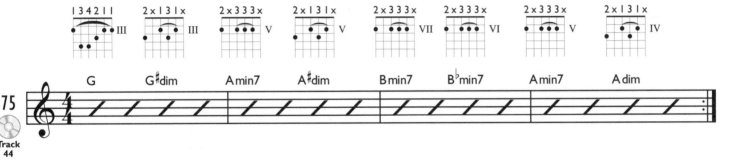

ROOT ⑤ CHORDS IN C

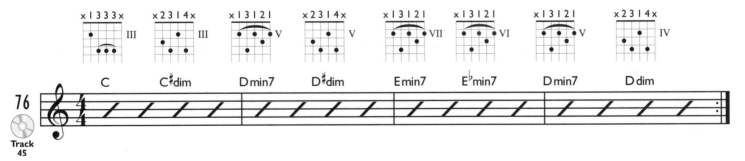

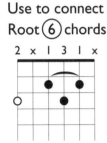

Track 44

Track 45

Dominant chords are often extended or altered to add color or to increase their tension or *leading* quality (the tendency to resolve to the tonic). The dominant 9th chord (9) is often used instead of the dominant 7th in rock music. The dominant 7#9 is also used extensively. A #9 is enharmonically the same as a ♭3 an octave higher and gives a chord a "bluesy" edge.

DOMINANT 9 CHORDS

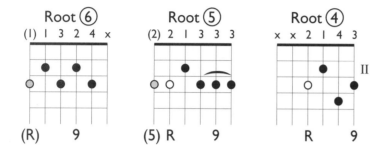

DOMINANT 7#9 CHORDS

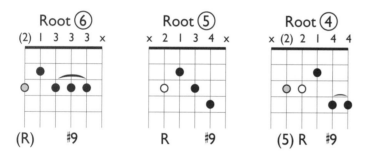

Another common sound in contemporary rock is the *suspended* (sus) chord. The most common suspended chord uses a 4th to replace the 3rd of a major chord. This is called a sus4 chord. It has a strong inclination to resolve back to the 3rd but is often used without resolving. This creates a very "open" sound. Listen to Andy Summers, The Edge and Eddie Van Halen for excellent examples of suspended chord usage. The two forms shown here are dominant 7th sus4 (7sus4) chords that are great for rhythm work. It is also an easy matter to raise the 3rd of any triad to the 4th to create a suspended chord. The suspended note is usually a 4th but can also be a 2nd (lower the 3rd one whole step).

DOMINANT 7sus4 CHORDS

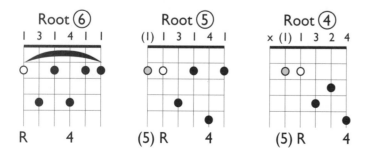

RHYTHMIC NOTATION

Rhythm guitar parts are usually notated in rhythmic notation in conjunction with chord symbols. It is helpful to clap or tap the rhythms before playing them. Examples 77 - 80 will give you some practice reading rhythmic notation. Pay close attention to the alternate picking (in this case, strumming) marks.

RHYTHMS IN ¾ TIME

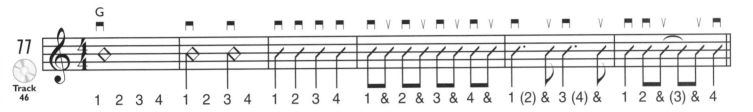

RHYTHMS IN ¾ TIME

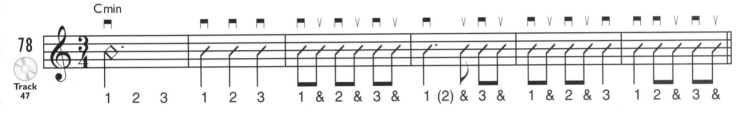

TRIPLETS

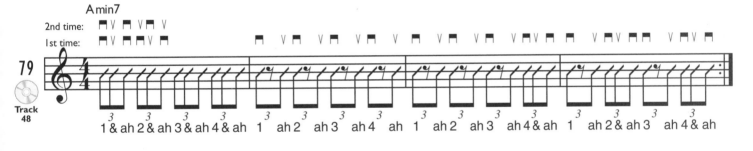

SIXTEENTHS

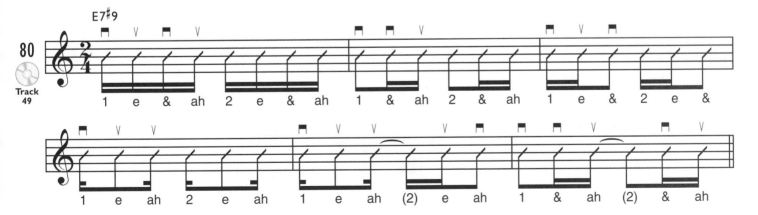

RHYTHM GUITAR EXAMPLES

The following examples are rhythm exercises that illustrate different "feels." Play through them to get an idea of how to incorporate your new chord forms and rhythms into a playing situation. Note the $\overset{\times}{}$ marks. These indicate a *chuck* or *cut*. Dampen the strings with your left hand while you strike the string to make a percusive effect.

You can also use these chord progressions to practice improvising. Play along with the CD or record them yourself. The shaded areas above each example will list the appropriate scales to use. All of the scales shown have been covered in *Beginning Rock Guitar* and in this book, with the exception of the Mixolydian and Dorian modes. If you are unfamliar with these modes, see Chapter 11 of this book.

BLUES IN A. Use A Minor Pentatonic. Notice the *turnarounds* at the ends of these blues examples. A turnaround creates a harmonic connection between the end of the blues form and the beginning. They are also sometimes used as introductions.

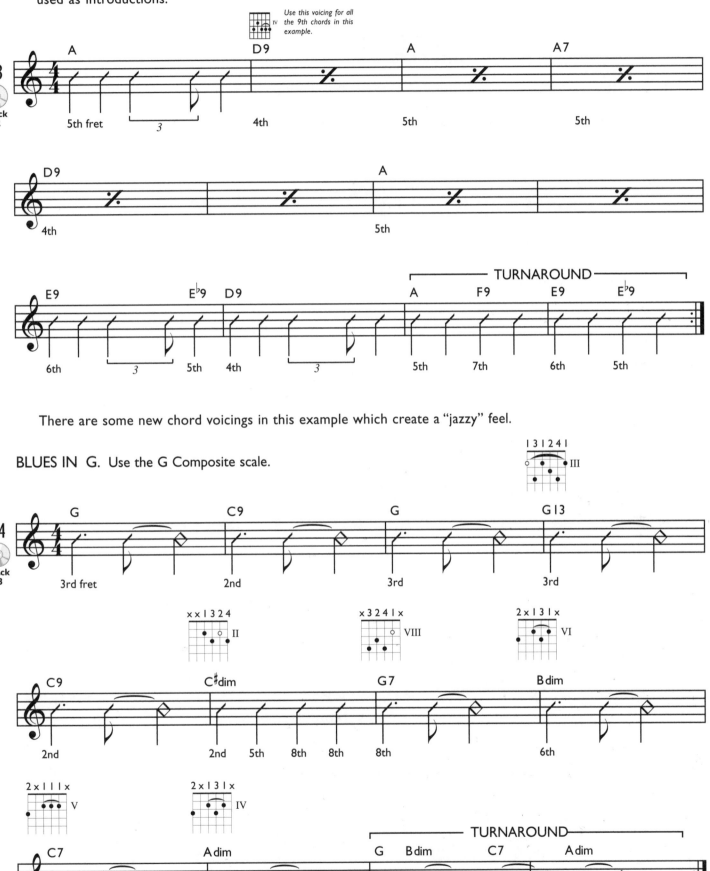

There are some new chord voicings in this example which create a "jazzy" feel.

BLUES IN G. Use the G Composite scale.

CHAPTER 10

Minor Scales

Like the major scale, a *minor scale* is a succession of tones in alphabetical order. A minor scale has a different quality because the sequence of whole and half steps is different. The most important characteristic of a minor scale is the ♭3. The most common minor scales used in rock are the *natural minor* and *harmonic minor* scales.

THE NATURAL MINOR SCALE

The natural minor scale, also known as the *Aeolian mode*, is a minor scale with the following sequence of whole and half steps:

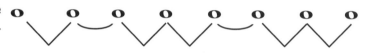

		= whole step
		= half step

PARALLEL MINOR SCALE

Another way to think of the natural minor scale is as a *parallel minor* scale. A parallel minor scale starts on the same root as a major scale, but has some alterations. This is where the numbering system comes in handy. If you lower the 3rd, 6th and 7th degrees of a major scale, you have a natural minor scale.

C Major	1	2	3	4	5	6	7	8
	C	D	E	F	G	A	B	C
C Natural Minor	1	2	♭3	4	5	♭6	♭7	8
	C	D	E♭	F	G	A♭	B♭	C

RELATIVE MINOR SCALE

This pattern can be created by playing the notes of a major scale, starting and ending on the 6th degree. The natural minor scale created this way is called the *relative minor* scale. For instance, if you play a C Major scale, starting and ending on the 6th degree (A), you will be playing the A Natural minor scale. So, A Natural Minor is the relative minor scale of C Major.

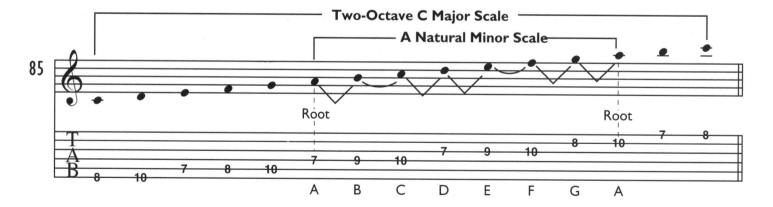

NATURAL MINOR SCALE FINGERINGS

Here is a basic one octave fingering for the A Natural Minor scale. Of course, you can move this fingering around the guitar to any root.

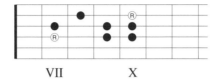

Here are seven useful fingerings for the natural minor scale. They are all shown in the key of A Minor, but you can move all of them to any root, except for the open position fingering. Most of them require you to shift (change positions). Notes in parentheses are alternate note locations that you can use if you would like to stay in one position.

Open Position

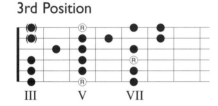

1st and 2nd Position

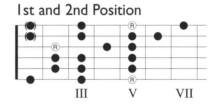

3rd Position

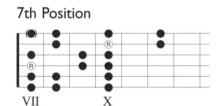

5th Position

7th Position

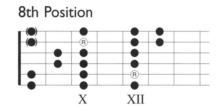

8th Position

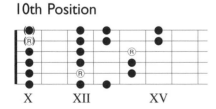

10th Position

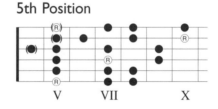

(●) = Alternative fingerings for playing in one position.

It is also important to note that the natural minor scale is an extension of the minor pentatonic scale (1 - ♭3 - 4 - 5 - ♭7). The natural minor simply adds the 2 and ♭6.

MELODIC PATTERNS IN A NATURAL MINOR

Try developing melodic patterns to practice the natural minor scale, just as you did with the major scale. For instance, try these patterns in all the different fingerings, in all keys, ascending and descending.

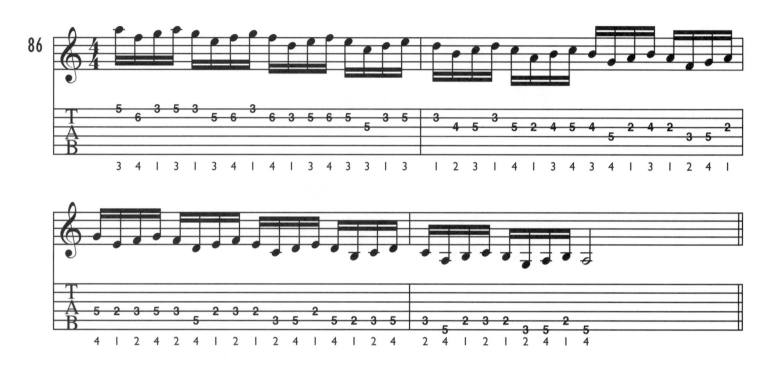

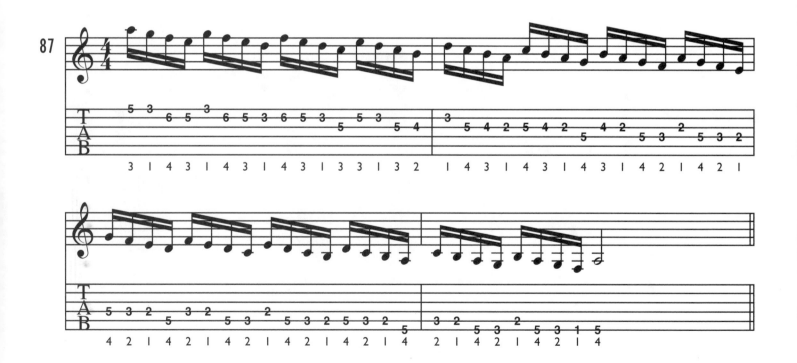

IMPROVISING WITH THE NATURAL MINOR SCALE

Here are two common chord progressions that you can use the natural minor scale to improvise over.

In A Minor

i	iv	v
Amin	Dmin	Emin

In C Minor

i	♭VII	♭IV
Cmin	B♭	A♭

Try playing the A Natural Minor scale over this one. Play along with the CD, or record the chords yourself, or get a friend to lay down the rhythm part. Enjoy!

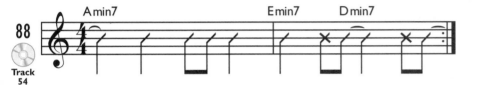

88

Track 54

It is interesting to examine the areas of the scale where the half steps fall. Playing around these areas can really bring out the character of the scale.

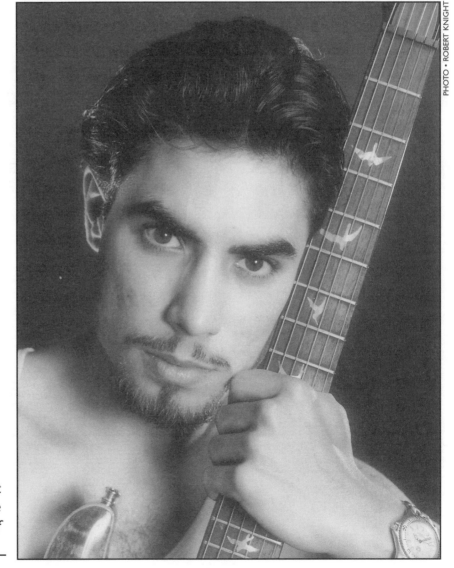

Dave Navaro
Guitarist for the Red Hot
Chili Peppers, Dave
Navaro is a master of
modern funk.

PHOTO • ROBERT KNIGHT

NATURAL MINOR LICKS

Here are some sample licks to help you get started using the natural minor scale. Use them for inspiration and make up some of your own.

A) A Minor, in the style of Marty Friedman

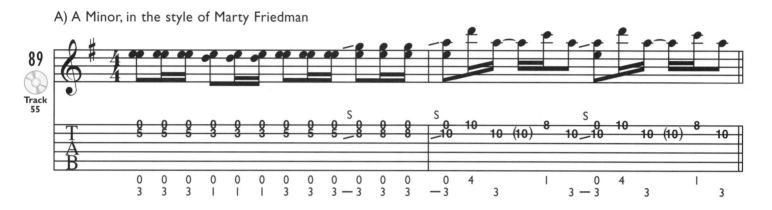

B) A Minor   C) B Minor

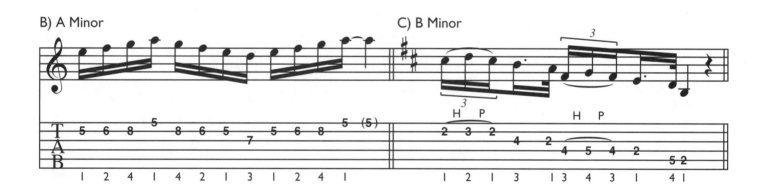

D) B Minor   E) G Minor

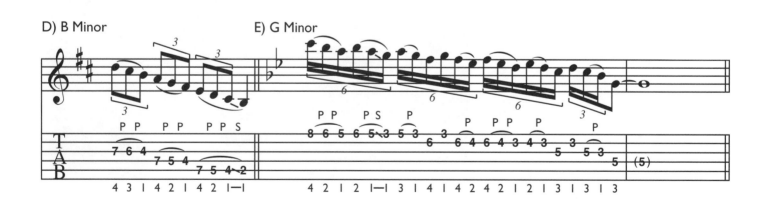

HARMONIC MINOR SCALE

The *harmonic minor* scale is a commonly used variation of the natural minor scale. It is an exotic sounding scale that is created by simply raising the 7th degree of the natural minor scale by one half step. This creates an augmented 2nd (1½ steps) between the ♭6 and ♮7.

Here is the formula for the harmonic minor scale:

| **I** | **2** | **♭3** | **4** | **5** | **♭6** | **♮7** |

Compare the A Natural Minor scale to the A Harmonic Minor scale.

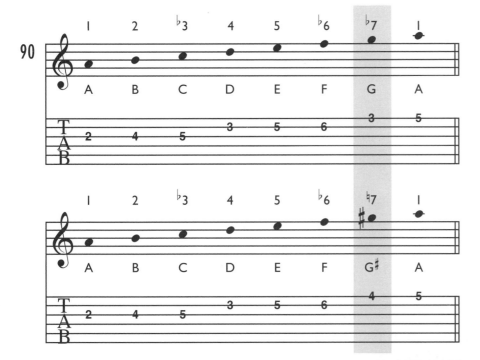

Eddie Van Halen
Van Halen's incredible tapping technique revolutionized rock guitar playing.

HARMONIC MINOR SCALE FINGERINGS

Open Position

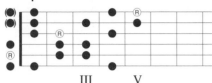

III   V

1st and 2nd Position

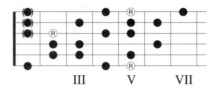

III   V   VII

3rd Position

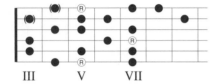

III   V   VII

5th Position

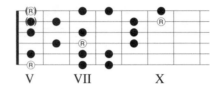

V   VII   X

7th Position

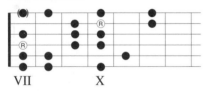

VII   X

8th Position

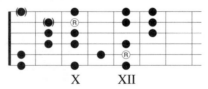

X   XII

10th Position

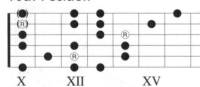

X   XII   XV

(●) = Alternative fingerings for playing in one position.

Try playing melodic patterns with the harmonic minor scale as you did with the major and natural minor scales. Do this in all the keys.

IMPROVISING WITH THE
HARMONIC MINOR SCALE

The harmonic minor scale is often used over a progression in which i and iv are minor but V is a dominant 7th chord. Here is a typical harmonic minor progression in E:

i	iv	V7
Emin	Amin	B7

The natural minor and harmonic minor scales are often used together for different parts of the same song. We can us the ♭7 over most chords, and the ♮7 over the V7.

Practice using both the harmonic and natural minor scales by playing over the examples provided on the next page. Play along with the CD that is availbele with this book. Or, record the examples yourself. Even better, find a friend to jam with!

Yngwie Malmsteen
The Paganini of rock guitar, Malmsteen uses the harmonic minor scale extensively.

Use D Natural Minor.

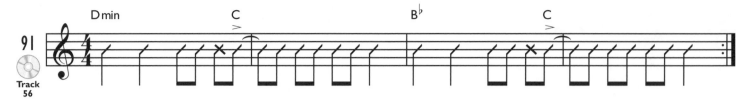

Use A Natural Minor.

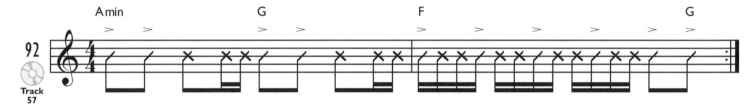

Use C Natural Minor, and C Harmonic Minor over the G7. Swing the eighths.

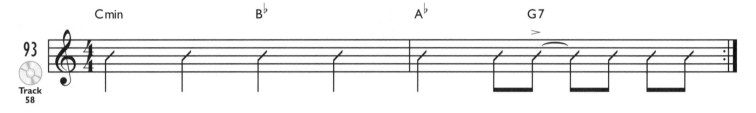

Use B Harmonic Minor.

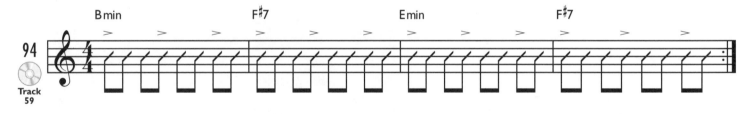

Use G Harmonic Minor. Swing the eighths.

HARMONIC MINOR LICKS

Here are some sample licks to help you get started using the harmonic minor scale. Try to make up some of your own.

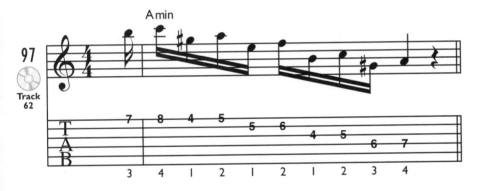

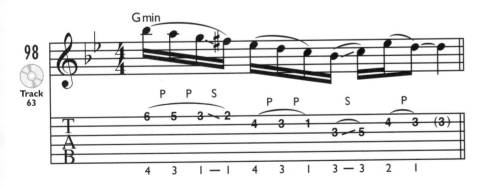

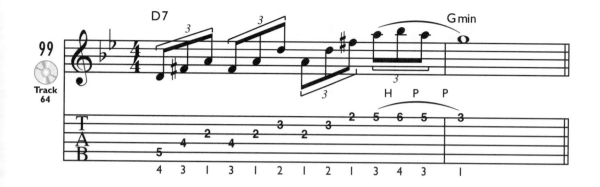

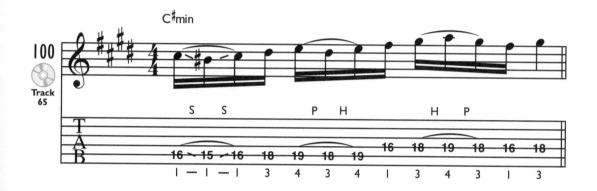

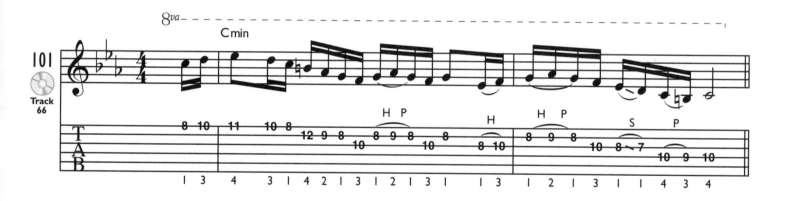

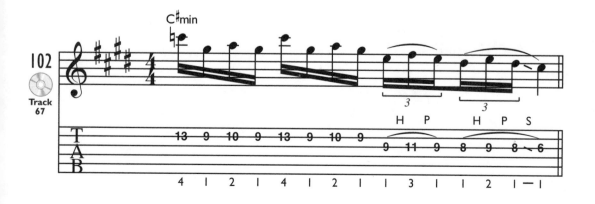

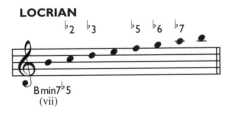

CHAPTER 11

The Modes

Every type of scale evokes a certain mood which is related to how the half steps fall in the scale pattern. The familiar major scale (also called the Ionian mode) has a "bright" or "up" feeling. The natural minor scale (Aeolian mode) that we examined in Chapter 10 has a more somber or "dark" quality.

By starting a scale from each note of the major scale, and using the same set of notes belonging to that major scale, we can create all the *modes* of the major scale. In other words, a mode is a re-ordering of the notes of a scale. This approach to viewing the modes is often called the relative approach. You can also view each mode as being parallel to a major scale of the same root. These are exactly the same concepts as the relative and parallel minor that you learned about in Chapter 10.

Besides the Ionian and Aeolian modes the two modes of the major scale most common to rock music are the *Dorian* and *Mixolydian* modes. These names come from the names of Greek tribes whose music was originally associated with these sounds.

The following example shows the modes of the C Major scale and the chord type most related to each mode. For instance, we think of a minor 7th chord as being closely related to the Dorian mode because that is the chord that results from building a diatonic 7th chord up from the root of the Dorian mode. The numbers above the scales refer to the parallel major scales and the alterations needed to get to the mode. For instance, if you lower the the 3rd and 7th degrees of a D Major scale (♭3 and ♭7) you will have a D Dorian mode.

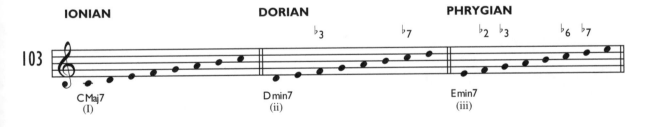

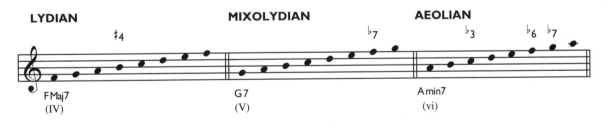

LOCRIAN

Bmin7♭5
(vii)

THE DORIAN MODE

The Dorian mode is a minor sounding scale. In the relative method of viewing the Dorian mode, it can be created by playing a major scale beginning on the 2nd degree. The mode can also be thought of with a parallel approach by remembering this formula:

$$1 \qquad 2 \qquad {}^{\flat}3 \qquad 4 \qquad 5 \qquad 6 \qquad {}^{\flat}7$$

Notice that, like the Aeolian mode (natural minor scale), the Dorian mode is simply an extension of the minor pentatonic scale (1 - ♭3 - 4 - 5 - ♭7). The Dorian mode simply adds the 2 and the 6.

Example 104 shows how an A Dorian mode can be derived from the G Major scale. Also, note the sequence of whole steps and half steps.

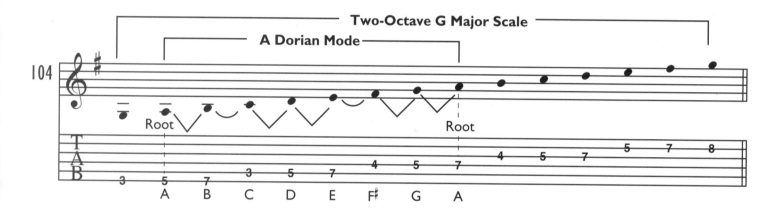

Carlos Santana
Many of Santana's best solos are based on the Dorian mode. Check out "Evil Ways" and "Black Magic Woman."

DORIAN MODE FINGERINGS

Here is a basic one-octave fingering for the A Dorian mode:

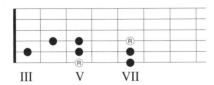

III   V   VII

Remember that this fingering can be transposed to any key by simply moving it to a different root. The diagrams below show seven three-note-per-string fingerings for the Dorian mode in A. The notes in parentheses are alternate fingerings for playing in one position (without shifting).

Open Position

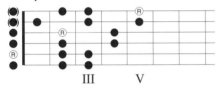

III   V

1st and 2nd Position

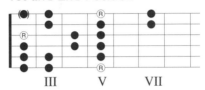

III   V   VII

3rd Position

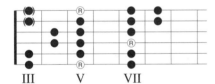

III   V   VII

5th Position

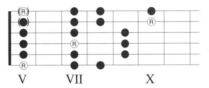

V   VII   X

7th Position

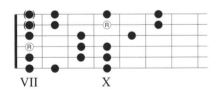

VII   X

8th Position

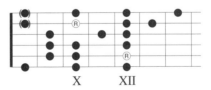

X   XII

10th Position

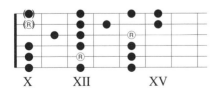

X   XII   XV

(●) = Alternative fingerings for playing in one position.

MELODIC PATTERNS IN A DORIAN

IMPROVISING WITH THE DORIAN MODE

Many players, such as Carlos Santana and Jimi Hendrix, have made extensive use of the Dorian mode. It can be used in several situations. Here are a few examples:

1. Over a progression that uses a minor i and a major or dominant IV, such as:

    i   **IV7**
Amin **D7**

2. Over a dominant chord. For instance, you can use E Dorian over E7, E9 or E7#9.

3. Over a blues progression to create a more "jazzy" sound.

Try improvising with the Dorian mode over these progressions. Pay attention to your *phrasing*—try to *resolve* your lines (bring them to rest) effectively.

Use G Dorian.

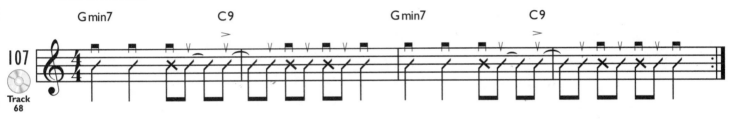

Use E Dorian.

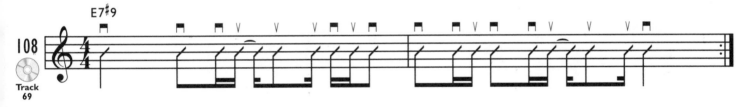

Use A Dorian.

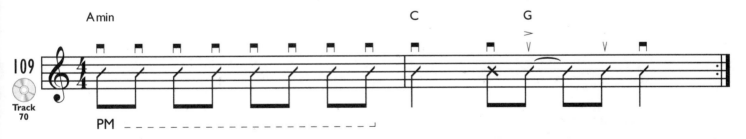

PM = *Palm Mute*. Rest the right side of your palm directly next to the bridge of the guitar to create a slightly deadened sound.

Use D Dorian.

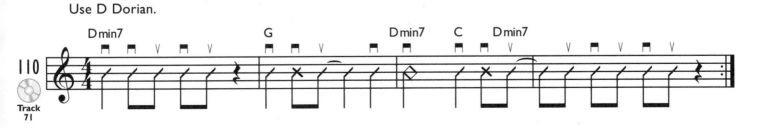

DORIAN LICKS

In the style of Danzig

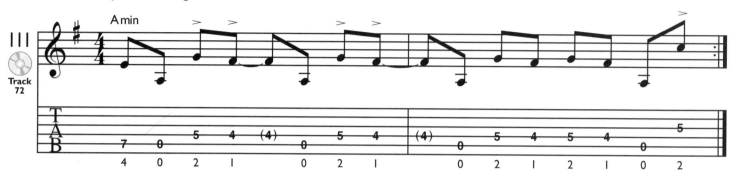

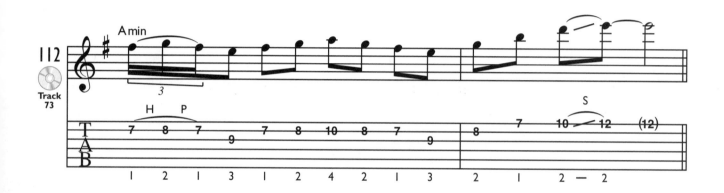

Swing the eighths.

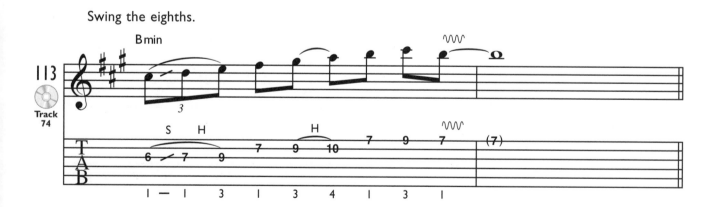

MAJOR PENTATONIC (R 2 3 5 6)

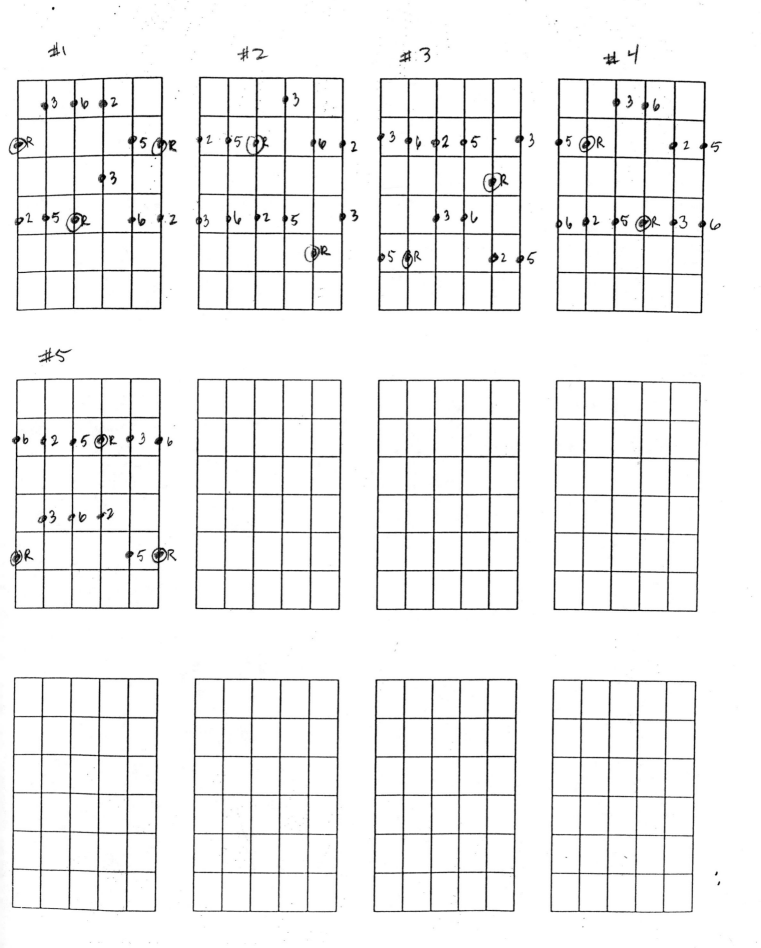

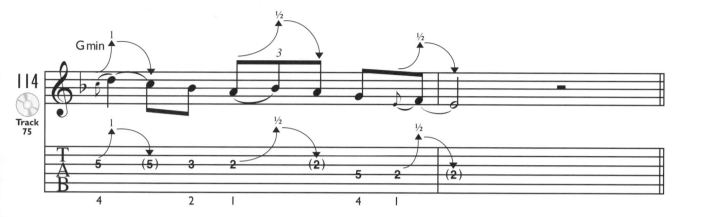

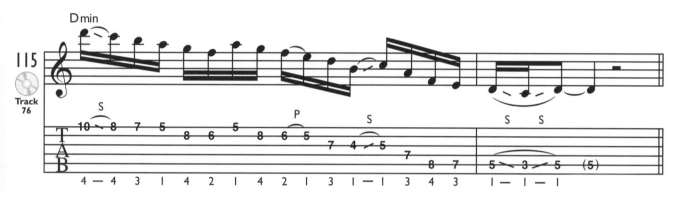

Swing the eighths in Examples 116 and 117.

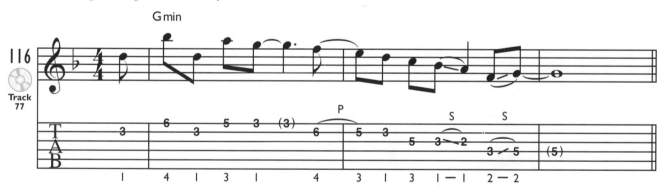

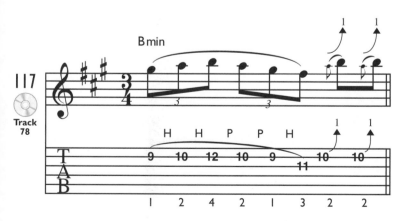

THE MIXOLYDIAN MODE

The Mixolydian mode is a major sounding scale. In the relative method of viewing the Mixolydian mode, it can be created by playing a major scale beginning on the 5th degree. The mode can also be thought of with a parallel approach by remembering this formula:

I	2	3	4	5	6	♭7

Notice that the Mixolydian mode is an extension of the major pentatonic scale (1 - 2- 3 - 5 - 6), as is the major scale itself. The major scale adds 4 and 7, the Mixolydian mode adds 4 and ♭7. The ♭7 gives the Mixolydian mode a dominant sound.

Example 118 shows how an A Mixolydian mode can be derived from the D Major scale. Also, note the sequence of whole steps and half steps.

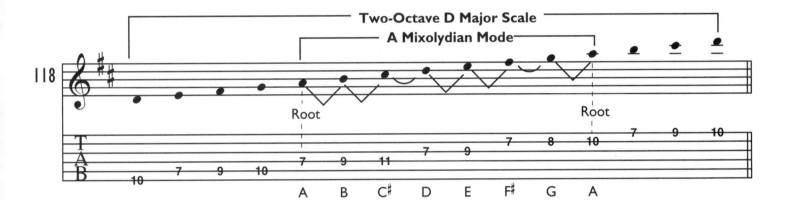

Jeff Beck
One of Beck's most enduring compositions, "Freeway Jam," is a Mixolydian classic.

MIXOLYDIAN MODE FINGERINGS

Here is a basic one-octave fingering for the A Mixolydian mode:

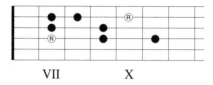

Remember that this fingering can be transposed to any key by simply moving it to a different root. The diagrams below show seven three-note-per-string fingerings for the Mixolydian mode in A. The notes in parentheses are alternate fingerings for playing in one position (without shifting).

Open Position

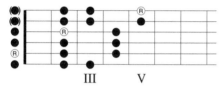

2nd Position

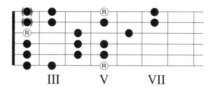

3rd Position

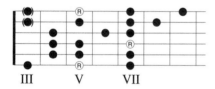

5th Position

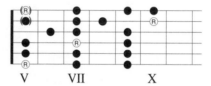

7th Position

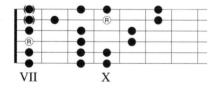

9th Position

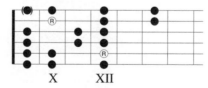

10th Position

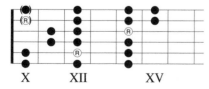

(●) = Alternative fingerings for playing in one position.

Adapt the melodic patterns given for the Dorian mode on page 78 to these fingerings for the Mixolydian mode. Then try creating some of your own. This is the best way to learn scale fingerings.

IMPROVISING WITH THE MIXOLYDIAN MODE

Here are a few examples of situations in which you can use the Mixolydian mode:

1. Over a dominant chord. For instance, you can use A Mixolydian over A7.

2. Over a progression that uses a I and ♭VII, such as:

I	♭VII
D	**C**

3. Over a blues progression when you are changing scales with every chord. For example, in an A blues:

I	/	IV	/	I	/	I	/	IV	/	IV	/
A7		**D7**		**A7**		**A7**		**D7**		**D7**	
A Mixolydian		D Mixolydian		A Mixolydian				D Mixolydian			

I	/	I	/	V	/	IV	/	I	/	V	//
A7		**A7**		**E7**		**D7**		**A7**		**E7**	
A Mixolydian				E Mixolydian		D Mixolydian		A Mixolydian		E Mixolydian	

John Lennon
His tune, "Norwegian Wood," a Beatle classic, is based on the Mixolydian mode.

Try improvising with the Mixolydian mode over these progressions. Remember to work on phrasing well. Pick out *target notes* on which to end your phrases. In other words, as you begin a phrase, have in mind the note you wish to end on, and direct your phrase towards that note. Target notes are usually chord tones. It is especially good to end phrases on a 3rd or 7th.

Use A Mixolydian.

Use F# Mixolydian.

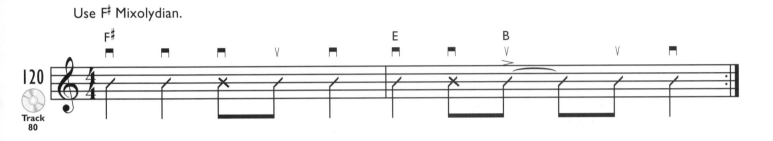

Use D Mixolydian.

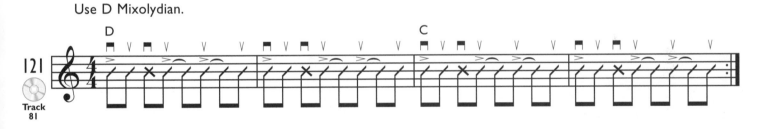

Use G Mixolydian.

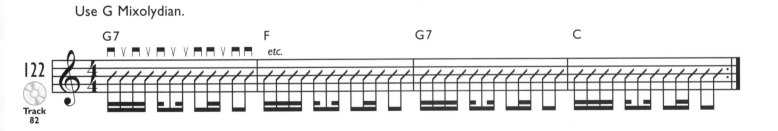

MIXOLYDIAN LICKS

In the style of Dave Matthews

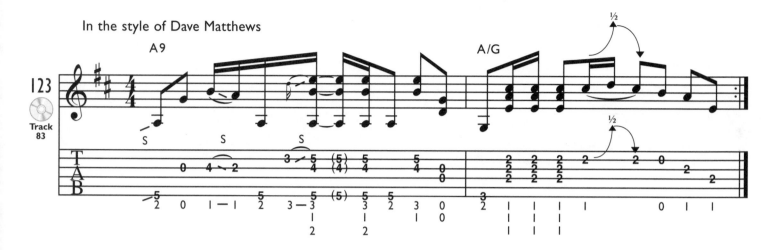

In the style of Jeff Beck

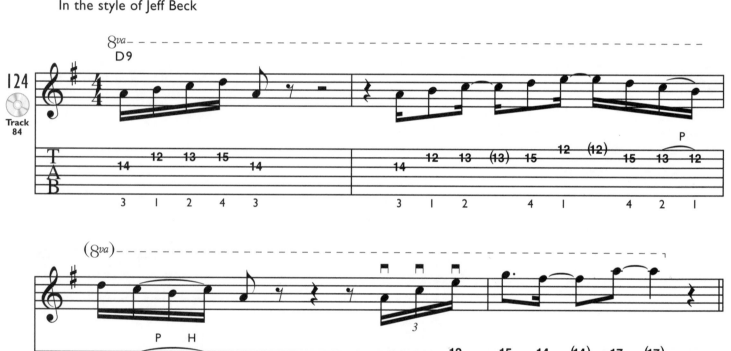

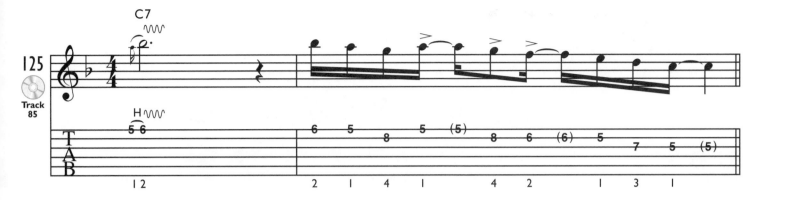

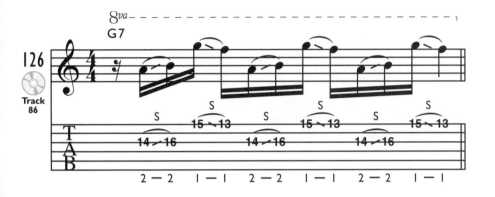

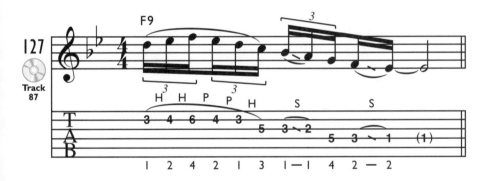

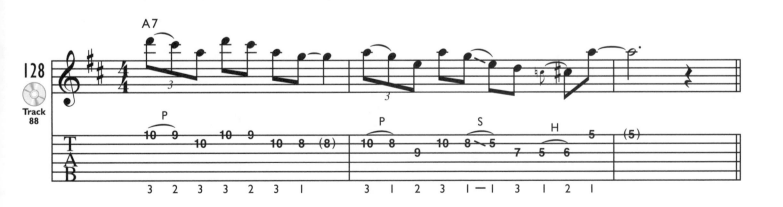

APPENDIXES

Appendix A—Scales and Modes

MODES IN THE NUMBERING SYSTEM

The table that follows uses the numbering system to compare all four of the modes you have investigated in this book. Notice that the first two, Ionian and Mixolydian, are major (have a ♮3); the next two, Dorian and Aeolian, are minor (have a ♭3). Also, notice that each mode has one more pitch alteration than the last. For purposes of easy comparison, all the scales and modes in this appendix will be shown in the key of A.

Ionian	1	2	3	4	5	6	7	1
A major mode. Identical to the major scale.	A	B	C♯	D	E	F♯	G♯	A
Mixolydian	1	2	3	4	5	6	♭7	1
A major or dominant mode.	A	B	C♯	D	E	F♯	G♮	A
Dorian	1	2	♭3	4	5	6	♭7	1
A minor mode.	A	B	C♮	D	E	F♯	G♮	A
Aeolian	1	2	♭3	4	5	♭6	♭7	1
A minor mode. Identical to the natural minor scale.	A	B	C	D	E	F♮	G♮	A

PENTATONIC SCALES IN THE NUMBERING SYSTEM

Continuing to use the numbering system to compare the scales, here are two pentatonic scales (major and minor) and the blues scale.

Major Pentatonic	1	2	3	5	6	
	A	B	C♯	E	F♯	
Major Pentatonic	1	♭3	4	5	♭7	
	A	C♮	D	E	G♮	
Blues Scale	1	♭3	4	♭5	♮5	♭7
	A	C♮	D	E♭	E♮	G♮

MINOR SCALES IN THE NUMBERING SYSTEM

Natural Minor *Identical to the Aeolian mode.*	1	2	♭3	4	5	♭6	♭7	1
	A	B	C	D	E	F♮	G♮	A
Harmonic Minor	1	2	♭3	4	5	♭6	♮7	1
	A	B	C	D	E	F♮	G♯	A

SCALES AND MODES IN STANDARD MUSIC NOTATION AND TAB

A IONIAN (A MAJOR)

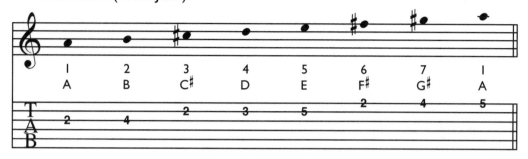

A MIXOLYDIAN

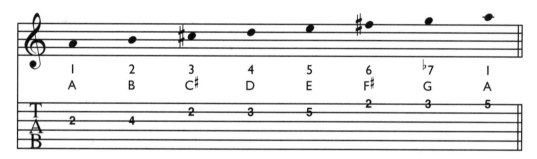

A DORIAN

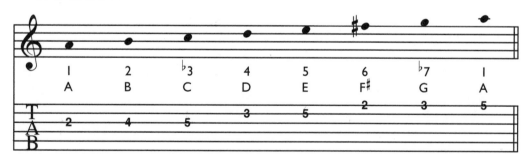

A AEOLIAN

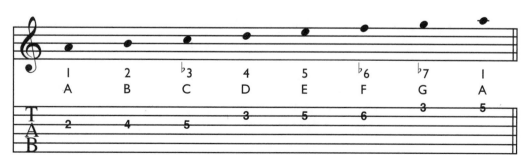

A MAJOR PENTATONIC

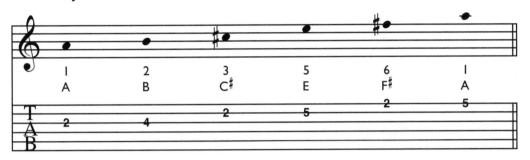

A MINOR PENTATONIC

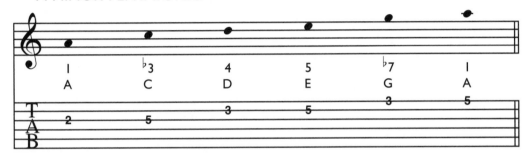

A BLUES SCALE

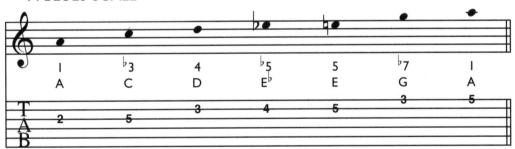

A HARMONIC MINOR

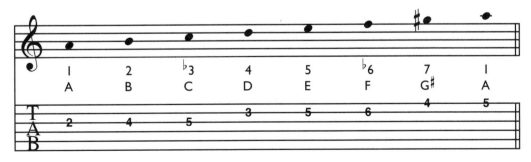

Appendix B—Suggested Songs for Practice

Major Scales
1. Always With Me, Always With You - Joe Satriani
2. Love Song - Tesla
3. Goodbye to Romance - Ozzy Osborne
4. Cliffs of Dover - Eric Johnson
5. Long Distance Run Around - Yes
6. Here Is No Why - Smashing Pumpkins
7. Gel - Collective Soul

Intervals
1. Keep On Growing - Derek & the Dominoes (Eric Clapton)
2. Brown-eyed Girl - Van Morrison
3. And the Cradle Will Rock - Van Halen
4. Soul Man - Sam & Dave (Steve Cropper)
5. Smoke on the Water - Deep Purple

Triads and Embellishments
1. Little Wing - Jimi Hendrix
2. The Wind Cries Mary - Jimi Hendrix
3. Panama - Van Halen
4. Any Rolling Stones song
5. Rock and Roll Hootchie Koo - Rick Derringer/Johnny Winter
6. Axis: Bold as Love - Jimi Hendrix
7. Life's Been Good To Me - Joe Walsh
8. Jimi Thing - Pearl Jam

Diatonic Harmony and Arpeggios
1. Hotel California - Eagles
2. Layla - Derek & the Dominoes (Eric Clapton)
3. While My Guitar Gently Weeps (the bridge) - The Beatles
4. Every Breath You Take - The Police
5. Spirit of Radio - Rush
6. I'll Be There For You - The Rembrandts
7. Glycerine - Bush

Composite Scales
1. T-Bone Shuffle - T-Bone Walker, Robert Cray
2. I Know a Little - Lynyrd Skynyrd
3. Rock & Roll - Led Zeppelin
4. Any Van Halen song
5. The Audience is Listening - Steve Vai
6. Midnight Express - Extreme

New Chords

1. You Know What I Mean - Jeff Beck
2. Stormy Monday Blues - Allman Brothers
3. Any song by Stevie Ray Vaughn
4. Hideaway - The Blues Breakers with Eric Clapton
5. Josie - Steely Dan
6. Warped - Red Hot Chili Peppers
7. Satellite - Dave Matthews Band

Natural Minor and Harmonic Minor

1. All Along the Watchtower - Jimi Hendrix
2. Stairway to Heaven - Led Zeppelin
3. Black Magic Woman - Santana
4. Any song by Iron Maiden
5. Europa - Santana
6. Any tune by Yngwie Malmsteen
7. In the Dead of the Night - Allan Holdsworth
8. Luminous Flesh Giants - Joe Satriani

Dorian Mode

1. Down by the River - Neil Young
2. In Memory of Elizabeth Reed - Allman Brothers
3. Moondance - Van Morrison
4. So What - Miles Davis
5. Any Blues tune
6. Oye Como Va - Santana
7. You - Candlebox

Mixolydian Mode

1. Reelin' in the Years - Steely Dan
2. Satch Boogie - Joe Satriani
3. Freeway Jam - Jeff Beck
4. Fire on the Mountain - Grateful Dead
5. I'm the One - Van Halen
6. Sweet Home Alabama - Lynyrd Skynyrd
7. Grind - Alice in Chains
8. What Would You Say - Dave Matthews Band

Appendix C—Essential Movable Chord Forms

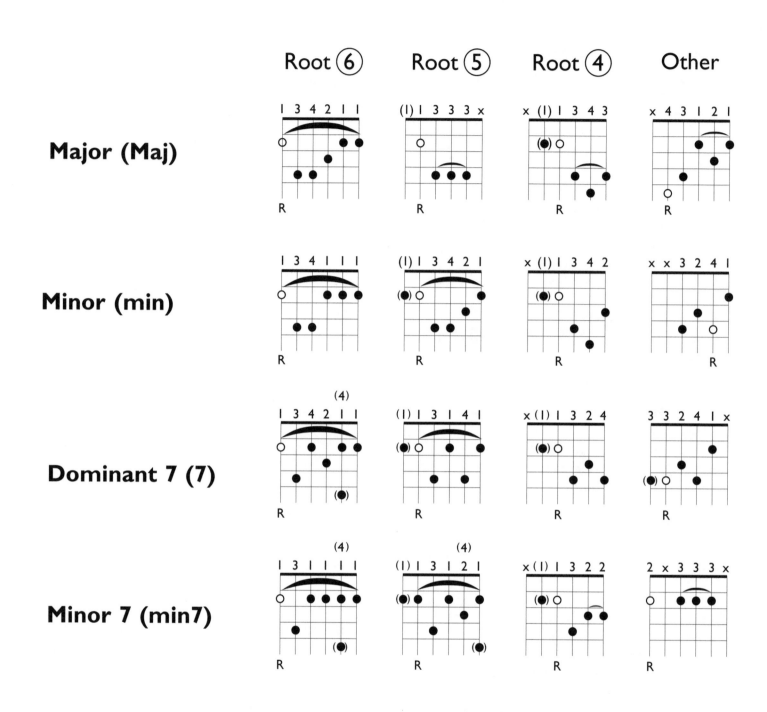

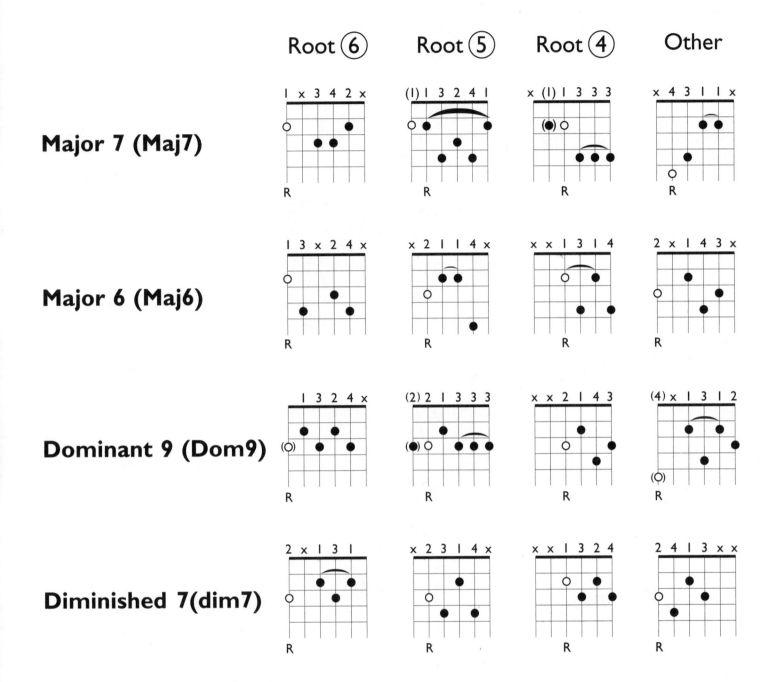

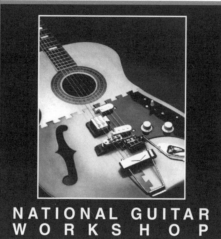